WARNING

If you are NOT interested in saving money and making more money;

If you are NOT interested in hiring and keeping the best possible employees;

If you are NOT interested in moving your workplace forward and making it great;

If you like to struggle everyday and maintain the *status quo* in a sometimes hostile workplace, then **stop reading now** and put this book down–it wasn't written for you!

On the other hand, if you are open-minded, willing to think outside the box, maybe even willing to consider unconventional ideas and concepts to make your workplace better, then READ ON!

As you read this book, you won't necessarily slap your knee, guffaw, and laugh out loud, but you will find out why you should want to–especially in the workplace.

This book will require you to open your mind and shift your thinking to a new direction. As you read this book, you will begin to look at your workplace in an entirely new way and discard your old beliefs. This book describes the secret ingredient to having it all in your workplace–and if you have been shopping for books about the workplace, you are most likely missing that secret ingredient.

If you are a business owner, get ready for greater personal satisfaction and professional success. If you are an employee in the workplace, then get ready to love your work. Once you learn to live the ideas presented here and contribute them to your workplace environment, all good things are possible!

Ann Fry

Laugh on! Ann 5/07

Laughing Matters

The Value of Humor in the Workplace

by Ann Fry

Laughing Matters:
The Value of Humor in the Workplace

2nd edition 2005

ISBN: 0-9646950-3-0

Library of Congress Control Number: 2003097284

The Better Way Press
P.O. Box 300567
Austin, TX 78703

Cover design by GRASP Enterprises
Book design by Print and Bind Direct!

Printed in the United States of America
Print and Bind Direct!
www.PrintAndBind.com

For information:
www.humoru.com

ACKNOWLEDGEMENTS

To Gabriel, my son, for always believing in me, encouraging me and being there for me. It is great to have an adult child as a mentor, who pursues his dreams and encourages me to fulfill mine.

To Betsy Chalfin, my sister, for being the best sister in the world, and always believing in me. And a special thanks for editing this material and making me "sound great" as a writer.

To Mark LeBlanc, Mary K. Marsden and all my coaches and mentors. Without a mentor and coach to kick me in the seat of my pants and push me to be all that I can be, this book would never have happened. "Thank you" is inadequate!

To the Landmark Education Community and my friends, especially Lee Follender, Linda Jones, and Terrill Fischer who sustain me, challenge me, love me and really fill me with possibilities. Thank you so much.

To all of my clients, who have trusted me and my work within their corporate structures. Thank you for believing in my work, allowing me to contribute to you and for being trail blazers in the *Fun at Work* movement.

To The Austin Business Journal, for publishing my column and believing in the concept of *Fun in the Workplace* for so many years!

Table of Contents

FOREWORD

My colleague, Ann Fry, has completed a much needed and humorous job in writing this book and it is a pleasure for me to write the foreword.

I am a professional comedian and improvisational performer, and have done a great deal of work in corporations around the country the past 10 years. I've had many trainers and academic friends who are really serious about telling me that humor and fun in the workplace are nice but not feasible. They say that people aren't looking for humor or fun; they just want to have a great environment in which to work. Excuse me, but doesn't having a work environment where people can laugh in both the good times and bad times show that you've got a good work environment? I've never seen or heard about a great work environment where everyone is really serious and no one laughs or smiles very much. Have you? Ann shows us how to look into the core of what goes into creating a truly meaningful work environment where laughter really matters. I have seen, on plenty of occasions, people laughing during one of my humor programs and they comment that they really needed to laugh and lighten up. When I asked why that was important to them, they responded that their work environment isn't fun, and everyone's too serious. The reality is that too few people are having fun at work. There is plenty of evidence (in addition to common sense) that suggests employees who can laugh and have fun at work also make more money for their employers. Just think...what if your customers could have a fun experience with your company? Wouldn't they want to come back and do more business with you? People at work really do want to enjoy their experience there and being able to laugh is important in that experience.

In this book, Ann brings a new perspective to the training and management arena. She provides practical guidance to managers and employees who have become aware that the chaos of the work environment requires that fewer employees must produce more results. The next wave of development is going to happen through the use of the human talent we have in our organizations. Ann is passionately committed to making that happen in her own unique and fun way. She's bringing the importance of humor back into work and showing you all the reasons why it's so vital to your business success. This book has lots of practical advice for transforming your place of business with the greatest tool that we all possess, our sense of humor. Ann has taught me, that ***"if all you do when you go to work is work, then you really need to LIGHTEN UP!"*** Simple but profound advice for us in these times of overwork and stress.

Ann practices what she preaches. She shares her wonderful sense of humor. You laugh. She connects with everyone and gets us all involved in ways that that get us laughing about our own foibles and the stressful things in our life. Like magic, she shows us that our stress disappears with our own laughter.

When you do business with Ann, you learn, you grow, and you laugh a lot. I applaud you for buying this book because you will now find out why "Laughing Matters!"

Terrill Fischer, Co-Founder & Dean of Humor at Humor University, Chief Entertainment Officer for *In The Moment Productions*

"It's no laughing matter, but it doesn't matter if you laugh!"

Jennie Gudmundsen

"It's bad to suppress laughter. It goes back down and spreads to your hips!"

Fred Allen

"A person has two legs and one sense of humor, and if faced with the choice, it's better to lose a leg."

Charles Lindner

INTRODUCTION

What humor intuits is hope in the midst of despair!
Dan Keller

"What's all this talk about a human in the workplace? Of course there are humans in the workplace. I mean, who else would be in the workplace? Animals? If there weren't humans in the workplace, nothing would get done..."

"Emily, that's *humor* in the workplace, not *humans*."

"Never mind!"

Those of you who are over 30, or anyone who watches *Saturday Night Live* reruns, will probably know that the dialogue came from Gilda Radner's character–Emily Latella. Emily was always misusing her words and causing confusion.

In this case, unlike Emily Latella, I'm here to create clarity; I'm here to talk about humor in the workplace and why we need it, must have it, will shrivel and die if we don't have it. I'm here to make the case that humor and fun in the workplace are absolutely and incontrovertibly necessary for all businesses that truly expect to succeed because, after all, **laughing matters!!!**

Gee, I wonder if they get it yet? Am I making myself clear here or am I the only one who gets it?

I've chosen to tackle this concept head on because I've grown weary of people in the workplace telling me that humor is insignificant, unimportant, frivolous, and unworthy of shallow pocket spending. To the contrary, I believe–in fact, I'm certain–that humor in the workplace is vital and, indeed, may be the single most important ingredient for workplace success and effective management. Yet, this secret ingredient is too often missing and I'd like to explore why it is missing and what we can do about it.

So, if you're ready to explore what will truly be a new concept for most of you, let's take the leap and begin our exploration. Here goes!

Leaping and exploring...what is this? A mountain climbing expedition?

You might have noticed some of my comments along the way...well, I'll be including them within (probably more for comic relief while writing this.) They might not mean anything to you, but to my bizarre thinking patterns, they're fun. They'll be in the margins like this, so you can always just skip over them!

The Magic Keys to the Kingdom

Wouldn't you like to have the magic *keys to the kingdom*? No, I'm not talking about Mickey's Magic Kingdom, but the keys that would open the door to a positively great, productive environment in the kingdom of your workplace. What do I mean?? I mean, what if you could actually ***know*** how to have the best possible workplace, earn the greatest amount of money possible, and be happy to boot?

What a concept?

It doesn't matter if you're a technician, a receptionist, an office manager, or a CEO–you just have to be someone who works for a living, for this information to be meaningful to you. Once you know what the *keys to the kingdom* are, here's what will happen:

All of your fellow employees will contribute to the productivity of your company.

Loyalty will be a given because everyone will know they are a valued and cherished member of the team.

The staff will be more creative and motivated.

Every employee in your company will look forward to the work day with enthusiasm and will find themselves participating wholeheartedly. You will be able to hire and retain the best, most productive employees and your staff will have your best interests in mind, every minute of every day.

I can just see the reader now rolling his/her eyes thinking I must be nuts to promise this.

Bottom line: Your company will be more profitable and successful; the best applicants will be knocking the doors down to get in because they will want to work for you–*you*, not XYZ Company across the street. Your staff will treat your customers with the kind of enthusiasm and respect that ensures repeat business. Your profits will rise, your stock will soar, your employee's bonuses will be well-deserved, you will be less stressed and feel more secure…Imagine! So, what is it that generates these professional riches? All of this is possible with a very simple formula: a willingness to *laugh* + *a sense of lightheartedness* = a *fun* and productive workplace.

Their eyes are really rolling now!

How do we get that formula in place? Where do we find those magic keys? First, really look at your workplace and the workday in a different way. How can you change your perspective and shift your paradigm?

Paradigm: If your employees are happy and have a full, fun-filled, balanced life, they will bring greater energy and enthusiasm to the workplace and your department, agency or company will function at peak performance.

Perhaps you have never thought of happiness as a necessary characteristic for your employees; but if I were to tell you that happy employees are more productive employees, would you be interested? If I could show you how a FUN and playful work environment boosts loyalty and performance without increasing your overhead, would you be interested in finding out how to create that environment? And, if I said that *laughing truly matters*, would you believe it?

I wonder how many times I'll have to try to convince them and if they'll get bored with how many times I say the same thing over and over? Oh, well, who knows if they're really reading this anyhow, they're probably just skimming through.

I'm inviting you to reconsider your workplace; expand your paradigm; look at what it means to have happy employees and a working environment where *fun is not out of place*. Once we've established the benefits of having happy, satisfied employees, we'll demonstrate how you can make your workplace more fun and *lighten up with humor.*

You must have heard the old adage, "Laugh and the world laughs with you..." So, let's explore the value of having happy employees who are capable of laughing in the face of potential adversity. Happy employees are more likely to:

- ✓ Appreciate the moment and go with the flow
- ✓ Take good care of themselves–physically and emotionally
- ✓ Have balance in their lives and have more focus
- ✓ Have a positive attitude and foster good relationships at work and outside of work
- ✓ Have a spiritual component in their lives that brings them joy
- ✓ Enjoy their work and all that life holds for them

Exercise:

Ponder, write down, and review your thoughts about the following question: How would a more positive fun work environment translate into a more effective workplace? [You might want to grab a colorful notepad and keep it as a journal for doing the exercises in this book.]

If you think "work" and "drudgery" are synonymous, you really need to lighten up! Think of the issues we face and the buzz words we use in our 21st century work world; words like change, downsizing, 24/7, doing more with less, re-engineering, conflict, stress, stress, stress...Employees have a lot of complaints. They don't think that management listens to their ideas, regardless of their experience, they don't feel appreciated or valued, they feel their jobs have no real purpose or connection to the bigger picture–in essence, they have no voice. As a result, there is greater substance abuse, higher absenteeism, more frequent job turnover, more anger and violence, more physical and emotional illness with subsequently soaring costs for healthcare.

So much for this being a lighthearted book

So, what can we do to change this picture? ***Lighten up, laugh, connect!***

Sounds too easy, right? But let's look at what it really takes to get there.

The work place has to be a pleasant destination. Let's look at current hiring trends in terms of people needs, not technical needs. Current research reveals a shift in hiring choices among Human Resource managers when assessing the personal characteristics of job applicants, especially for leadership roles. Technical skills are no longer number one. Topping the list of desired qualities are people skills–also known as "soft skills," newly termed, "emotional intelligence." The traits that recruiters look for include; good listening skills, good verbal and non-verbal communication skills, rapport building, empathy, socialization skills, authenticity, and, you guessed it, a sense of humor. In the enlightened workplace of the 21st century, the focus is on how best to *involve* leaders on a person-to-person level, and employees are viewed as the company's most important customers.

I don't know about them, but I'm yawning. Hope I start to make this more interesting … soon.

If we keep our employees happy, they will take good care of our customers. A lot of evidence supports this hypothesis, evidence based on my experiences working with a number of major corporations and evidence documented by the masters and wise people of the world. Soon, I'll be sharing some of this information and I will provide exercises for you to expand your own thinking. Most importantly, I will present concrete criteria of *what humor in the workplace looks like* so you'll know it when you see it.

Are you ready? Let's explore the possibilities and have some fun!

**"Congratulations!
Today is your day.
You're off to Great Places!
You're off and away.**

**You have brains in your head.
You have feet in your shoes.
You can steer yourself
Any direction you choose.**

Dr. Seuss

ONE

Laughing Matters...
It Really Does
or
The BIG WHY–
The Rationale
or
WHY It Matters Anyway

I couldn't decide on an actual chapter title here, so I used them all.

People who laugh together are less inclined to kill one another.
Conrad Hyers

I remember the first time I heard the expression, "laughing matters," I didn't get it. Did it mean that there were matters related to laughing? Or did it mean that laughing means something? Well, I think it's both. It really seems to make a difference, or *it matters* when people laugh; and there definitely *are* matters related to laughing.

Now, let's explore how *laughing matters* in your workplace. Close your eyes and visualize walking through your company's corridors.

Now how exactly can they close their eyes and still be reading this exercise and doing it? Well, they're smart people, they'll figure it out.

It's quiet, maybe *too* quiet. You peek into offices and all you see are people staring at computers, typing away, or perhaps speaking quietly on the telephone. Maybe a few employees are passed out at their desks, sleeping! You pass others as you walk through the corridor and they nod, but you notice they have serious facial expressions or, perhaps, even scowls. You walk into the restroom to wash your hands and glance in the mirror–you see that your face looks like all the others–grim! You spend an entire day retracing your steps, but the picture never changes. How do you feel at the end of this day? Happy with your work environment? Energized? Hardly. Worn out? Depressed? Frustrated?

Now, let's recreate this vision. Close your eyes and visualize walking through your company's corridors. As you pass others, they nod and smile at you; they greet each other with smiles and amusing gestures,

---

I said amusing...not any other kind of gestures.

---

ultimately generating laughter, snorts, chuckling, snickering, etc. You peek into people's offices and you see them smiling while on their phones, talking in an animated, upbeat manner; you even see them sitting back while they look at their computer screens–they are thinking and creating! How do you feel at the end of this day? Energized? Absolutely. Perhaps you're even reluctant to leave your office. When you do leave, you walk out with some of your co-workers and everyone is telling jokes, sharing anecdotes, and enthusiastically talking about tomorrow and finishing the project you have all been working on. The camaraderie and positive energy are palpable. You like–maybe even *love*–where you work.

I'm sure using the "L" word (love) is getting an interesting reaction about now.

If you are a manager or the CEO, you are delighted that your employees are happy and enthusiastic about their work…

Right!

…creative juices are flowing freely. Wow! Not bad. And this difference seems to stem from one thing–a sense of lightheartedness and good humor.

That's just the *personal* side of this story. Yes, *laughing matters,* but what about the professional advantages? How is your company or your workplace affected by a different attitude among the staff?

Studies show that we spend 75% of our time in work-related activities! So, if we spend 75% of our time somehow involved in work, how do we want it to go? How do we take work that now seems boring and find a way to do it that will actually make it interesting?

Man, it's gonna be tough pulling this one off… how will I convince them that I know the answer to that?

Author's note

I was a psychotherapist for 25 years. During those 25 years, people who were really stressed out or depressed and miserable about their jobs constantly called me for appointments. It became such a common thread throughout my therapeutic work, that I decided to give up my individual therapy practice so that I could work directly with companies and impact the work culture, thus helping many more people. Now, I am an advocate for creating more positive workplaces so that all of us who work can feel better.

Yes, I suppose this has become my mission...to right the woes wrought upon people in the workplace...to dream the impossible dream, to fight the unbeatable foe...Yes, I wanted to become the Woman of *La Mancha*, but my windmills became overly-serious executives and the corporate culture. I started to poke around those quiet corridors to see what was really going on behind closed doors and I began to survey employees to find out how they really felt about their work. What I learned astonished me and astonishes me still. The windmills are bigger than I could have imagined and they fight back when someone like me tries to turn them in a different direction. So, I decided that if I couldn't change them over with serious intent, then, by gosh, I'd bowl them over with humor.

Gosh, what if the reader never saw Man of la Mancha and has no clue about the whole windmill thing? They'll think I'm really weird. Oh well, I just have to take that chance.

How humor benefits the company

You are beginning to see that laughter really does matter to us, personally. But how is this of benefit to your workplace and, ultimately, your own career?

Consider some of the actual results we have seen when our hypothesis has been applied in the corporate setting.

Say a company experiences a boost in productivity, in some cases by as much as 50%. If you are normally skeptical, you might wonder, *if* that is so, *why*?

☺ When people are happy, they have more energy and they automatically *do* more. A happy individual feels energized and is less likely to procrastinate. The "to do" piles stacked high on desks disappear more quickly; sales calls get made more quickly and, since we all know that enthusiasm is contagious, more deals are closed more quickly.

$ The bottom line: Greater productivity means more income for the company; with a little humor, you "blow the lid off" your productivity!

☺ In a positive work environment where employees are considered and appreciated, where loyalty and creativity are greeted enthusiastically, they do not want to leave.

$ Higher retention rates save companies a lot of money. It is estimated that the cost of hiring and training a new employee is nearly equivalent to a full year's salary. So, clearly, a happy staff stays, all benefit from continuity and shared experience, and the company prospers.

☺ Customer service is a positive concept instead of an anxiety-ridden chore. Customers subconsciously internalize the general mood and morale of company employees. We are all more likely to deal with a company whose employees acknowledge our concerns, anticipate problems, and solve problems when they occur.

☺ When fun and lightheartedness are encouraged during the normal course of the workday, employee morale is high; teamwork is the norm; attitudes are positive; energy is tremendous; staff members are energized and enthusiastic; creativity flows.

$ Positive energy translates into more business. Think of all the times you have telephoned a company to inquire about a product. Think of your interactions with the customer service representatives. Were they pleasant and enthusiastic? Did they sound interested in answering your questions or solving your problem? Would you do business with them again? If your experience was not so good, did you consider why it wasn't?

A happy employee with a good sense of humor projects a positive attitude to your customers. A positive attitude is contagious and encourages repeat business. More business = ? You know, more business = more money.

Creativity flows like champagne. Productivity is at a peak. In an environment where humor is a vital component of the organizational structure, ideas are generated with ease and frequency. Consider the possibilities. Perhaps a new product line? Perhaps a new service!

Whatever new directions a company takes, if the employees support it enthusiastically, the atmosphere becomes electric. Employees are more dedicated and work harder. More business is generated. More business = ...you know...

Absenteeism rates decline precipitously. In a positive work environment, there is a greater sense of involvement and enjoyment at work. Stress-related illnesses decline. Employees are much less likely to need or take that "mental health" day. Watch health-related expenses decrease. Better attendance contributes to increased productivity. Less absenteeism clearly saves a lot of money. Less overhead expense for temporary staff + greater productivity from permanent employees = more *money*.

That's a "no-brainer!"

During the course of the workday, more work is being accomplished. When employees are in positive spirits, the gates of communication open wide. Employees actually enjoy the ping pong of work-related brain storming over the water cooler. When communication improves, there is greater trust; less need for clarifying and looking over one's shoulder.

More communication means more is accomplished in the same period of time. That means....Hello!! Do I hear the distant sound of, "*Ka ching*!"

Ka ching... now that's a really nice sound. I hope they know the word.

We could go on and on forever about the financial benefits of humor and lightheartedness in the workplace. So, you see, ***laughing matters***! It really makes a difference. It works!

Yeah, but when the boss makes more money, is she sharing it with those that help her make it...I certainly hope so.

The second half of this chapter focuses on *laughter*. Yep, that's right–laughing!! So, what's the payoff when people laugh?

Do you know that medical studies show there are real physiological advantages from laughter? When we laugh, lots of physical things happen:

☺ Our arteries dilate, which is great for the heart
☺ Respiration improves; we actually breathe better

Breathing is a good thing!

☺ Internal organs are massaged as the diaphragm convulses.

So, who doesn't like a massage?

☺ The body releases toxins–tears fall when we laugh a lot and so we get to cleanse the toxins right out.

- ☺ The immune system is affected positively. A healthy immune system really improves our overall health and longevity.
- ☺ Endorphins run wild–the body's own natural little pain-killers and "feel good hormones" explode.

Yowie!!

The author, Norman Cousins, was diagnosed many years ago with a potentially terminal illness. He decided to watch cartoons, comedies, Marx Brothers movies…anything that would make him laugh. His book *Anatomy of an Illness* describes the evolution of his illness and how he survived it. He refers to laughing as internal jogging! It's like non-impact running, and it only happens inside of your body. Who could ask for a better–and less sweaty–workout? (More about this in a minute).

Besides, I actually like the internal jogging better than the running because then my legs don't ache.

Paradigm: All in all, things are better—even great—in a workplace where LAUGHING MATTERS. Does that mean we should be constantly laughing? Of course not...but more, rather than less...that's significant.

So what does it take to have that kind of workplace? Well, that's food for thought, and the continuation of our story in the next chapter. So, your second assignment is to start looking *and listening* around the corridors and offices where you work. If it's a happy place and laughing matters…great. If not, start laughing and shift your consciousness. Yes, *YOU*! You can shift the consciousness…the culture. Yes, you can! You'll be amazed at how easy and contagious it can be.

Misery

I have one over-arching key concern. **Too many *people are MISERABLE (not merely unhappy, but MISERABLE) in their workplaces.*** Most employees feel overwhelmed, overworked, under-appreciated, and totally insecure. Every day, as they drive to work, a lot of people wonder if this will be the day they will be axed, or *downsized,* or, even worse, will this be the day their co-worker is cut loose so that they will have to do the work of two people?

If people spend 75% of their day involved in work-related activity, then the workplace ***should*** be a great place to be. If, instead, people are miserable because they are in a hostile, alien environment, people *and* their companies suffer. This seems pretty easy to follow, don't you think?

Now, it seems obvious to me–and I hope to you–that having a more lighthearted and fun workplace makes sense–it's a "*no brainer*". However, it is still a mystery to many folks. Once you begin to talk about the concepts you learn in this book, you will find that some people will not have a clue about what you're talking about. You are going to have to go out on a limb or two and take some risks to create a positive workplace in which to work. You will find, as I have, that taking those risks is well worth the return.

Think about starting a *fun committee* and choose activities that people will love. Get the people at the top to buy-in to your plan. Use some of the facts I present here to persuade them that they will see increased productivity–remember, *ka ching...*that should get their attention. What we are presenting is a *win/win* opportunity. Once staff and management begin to see even the earliest improvements in morale, everyone will want to get on the bandwagon–great results have that effect on people!

Of course the unspoken here is that the boss will have to cough up some money for the activities. Hope the boss is generous!

The power of positive thinking

A happy person is not a person in a certain set of circumstances, but rather a person with a certain set of attitudes. *Hugh Downs*

So, how can we be more playful at work? Is it even appropriate to be playful at work? Those are the questions we must answer if we want to get those magic keys.

When I approach a prospective client and tell them about what I do, I have to be *really* prepared–not just prepared with my presentation materials, but prepared to sell the benefits of fun and lightheartedness in the workplace–before I even get to my presentation. At the outset, many corporate executives think of *fun in the workplace* as frivolous–is it? *Not!*

I mean, it's not like I'm telling people to go and swing from the rafters or shoot craps...I'm just suggesting a little silliness.

Think about how being playful benefits you as a person. For example, how does it affect your attitude? For most of us, it dispels a lot of negativity and generates more positive thinking. Once we feel more positive, we banish pessimism and head off on an optimistic track. When we generate optimism and "positivity", it draws people toward us–we are someone more likely to have people around us–we become magnetic. Think about it–most play involves others, like team sports, party games, a game of Monopoly. Children learn sportsmanship and team building skills through play. So, playfulness and lightheartedness set the stage for greater possibilities and great relationships in our lives.

Besides, magnets are really cool and I myself prefer a cup half full!

How else does being playful benefit us? Play often leads to laughter. Clearly, we know the benefits of laughter in improving health and a sense of well-being. Laugh out loud for a few minutes and you exercise almost every part of your body–it stands to reason then that we will have more energy and, very likely, better mental and physical health.

And, duh, more productivity … ka ching!

Exercise:

Try it—right now. Just start laughing. Envision something really funny that you saw or something funny that happened to you and start laughing out loud—a real belly laugh—and see what happens. Remember the list of the physical effects of laughing that we included earlier? Did you feel any of them? Write about what happened in your journal. If you thought of something really hilarious that made you laugh, write about that too, so you can remember it and laugh every time you think about it.

Now, let's translate what we have learned so far to playfulness in the workplace. Ask any CEO or upper level manager what's important to them in the workplace. Most likely, their first concern will be about productivity and bottom-line profits. Then, they may go on to talk about turnover rate, employee retention, reducing the cost of health benefits, how to improve communication, and reduce absenteeism and stress...You get the idea. Then, ask them if they are concerned about whether or not the employees are happy at work. Most often, in my experience, the most frequent response to that question is that productivity is the goal–employee happiness is something they haven't thought about. But therein lies the rub! If you want better productivity, you need to "up" the happiness quotient! They go hand-in-hand. Now that we have embarked on the search for the magic keys to the kingdom, it is a new part of our jobs to focus our colleagues and our higher-ups on a new concept–fun in the workplace! That is how productivity will be achieved.

Paradigm: Focus on happiness and playfulness because that is how you will achieve the results you want! A happy employee is truly a productive employee.

Use this list as your mantra when "selling" the idea of humor in the workplace.

Happy employees are:

- absent from work less frequently
- less likely to quit their job
- apt to exhibit less stress and reduce consumption of health care
- more productive!

Paradigm: Playfulness injected into your company can only generate benefits to you. Playfulness is like a good, safe, legal drug —- and it's free!

Exercise:

Ask yourself and write down in your journal: How happy/playful is my workplace? What can I do to make it more fun? How will it help our bottom line? If you are a CEO or a manager: Ask yourself how you can afford *not* to have a playful/happy work environment?

Take this test

How do the people in your office see their work environment – as fun or a drag?

Do your co-workers spend a big part of their workday feeling bored and unproductive, even though they may actually do their jobs well? Do these same coworkers spend their down-time calling friends who are bored at their workplaces, too? If your answer to any of these questions is, "yes," are you willing to teach your co-workers the concepts of *fun in the workplace*?

Like, isn't that why they're reading this book??

So, what's a company to do?

Experts say laughter is likely the cheapest medicine. What a concept! Think of it–corporate employees daring to reveal their funny side. To implement laughter or a lighthearted atmosphere, some common misconceptions need to be clarified and a lighter approach learned. There is seldom a quick fix for the stoic office or the cardboard boss.

Social researchers have looked at why happy workers are more productive. This is what they have found:

- Having fun gives employees an effective way of releasing tension, and allows them to concentrate on their work more efficiently.

- A good laugh counteracts boredom and reduces personal conflicts.
- Interacting enjoyably with co-workers reduces the need to get social support outside of the workplace by calling home, goofing off with friends, or staying away from work. So, it seems that being able to laugh on the job does go hand in hand with increased productivity.

Do I need to say more?

There is a general misconception that if employees are having a good time and laughing, they must be goofing off. The key is being serious about work and problem solving, but not taking yourself so seriously. The goal is to use playfulness and humor to help relieve stress in the workplace, not to develop stand-up comedians.

The important question to answer is, ***Is the work being done?*** If it is, then why shouldn't the people doing the work have a good time while they are doing it?

The answer is a simple one. Using humor as a valuable tool in management is not about *being funny*–it is about developing a sense of humor, appreciating the value of humor, and applying the positive energy created by humor to enhance communication skills and strengthen a manager's persuasive power.

Think about Southwest Airlines. Their goal is not to make people laugh–it is to make money for their stock holders by providing a successful transportation service. By adopting a philosophy of *fun,* they have created an environment in which laughter is welcome. By welcoming laughter and fun, Southwest management has opened their arms to ambition, initiative, high morale, high productivity, and low turnover among employees, while creating incredible loyalty among their customer base. This is a brilliant leadership style, which has resulted in great success for the airline.

Here's a story about a flight I was on recently:

Late one evening on a westbound flight, one of the passengers became irate–in fact, let's refer to him as *TIP*. He began the flight in a surly mood. A few minutes following lift off, *TIP* pushed the flight attendant button and demanded a drink immediately. The flight attendant promptly delivered a drink. A few minutes later, *TIP* pushed the button again to complain that there was too much ice in his drink. Again, the flight attendant accommodated *TIP* and exchanged the drink. Passengers sitting nearby began to feel uncomfortable; *TIP* was so annoying that he was becoming disruptive. The flight attendant went on about her duties distributing peanuts and drinks to other passengers. Again- you guessed it–*TIP* pushed his button. The flight attendant approached and asked how she might help, never revealing any inkling of annoyance. *TIP* said, "These peanuts are bad!" She extended her left hand to collect the "bad" peanuts. She placed them in her palm. As she held the peanuts in her left palm, she pointed at them with her right forefinger and scolded them with the admonition, "Bad peanuts!"...shaking her finger at them. *TIP* couldn't maintain his annoyance any longer and cracked up, along with everyone else around him.

Moral: Humor diffused an angry, potentially escalating, episode and saved the day ... or the flight, in this case!

The key to making humor work for any company is to help employees understand the goal and improve their own humor and coping skills.

Paradigm: Happy employees are more creative, show more motivation and work more cooperatively in teams as they help your company move forward toward it's mission.

"It is almost inhumane if companies create a climate where people can't naturally have fun…Our role and responsibility as leaders and associates is to create a place where people can enjoy themselves. I know our company is doing well when I walk around and hear people laughing." Hal Rosenbluth, CEO of Rosenbluth International

Preaching to the choir

You, the readers, are the choir, and I'm probably preaching here.

Of course, by now they are probably beginning to believe in this stuff but I'll preach anyhow–think of it as sharing information.

An interesting thing is happening at American companies these days. From very small companies to Fortune 500 corporations, businesses are actually beginning to listen to some of the principles I'm speaking to you about here, and they are actually learning to put fun into work. In fact, many companies are using the word "humor" (or some variation) in their mission or value statement–Some companies even have a "Humor Consultant" on staff!

When I first visit a company that has asked me to talk to them about my program, my first question is, "Who is the designated FUN person here?"

Does *your* company have one?

There is an underlying assumption that humor, laughter, or a playful attitude on the job will be viewed negatively in most corporations. When you talk to employees privately (both managers and staff), they almost always say that they have to be careful about letting their sense of humor show on the job. (It's like they have to tiptoe around the issue….. shhh!) Both staff and management fear that people will interpret humor as being unprofessional or, worse, that they are incompetent or not taking their jobs seriously. Often, management makes the assumption that being playful or having fun results in less productivity.

We have already demonstrated that productivity increases with humor. But let's talk about it for a minute.

Yes, again!

Let's say you take a break and have a lighthearted conversation with a co-worker, or listen to a joke, or read a funny cartoon that someone has put on the bulletin board in the corridor. Do you think you'll return to work feeling more or less refreshed? Clearly, you'll feel *more* refreshed–you've generated some energy and activated your brain; you return to your office in a better mood. So, what does that mood do to your productivity? Increases it, of course!

I rest my case. Of course, if it was my break, I'd also like a few Hershey's kisses, too.

Paradigm: The word is out—employees who enjoy their jobs work more effectively. As a result, companies see a significant difference in the bottom-line with decreased employee turnover and increased morale and team-work.

Authors Note

I'm working with a company that, according to the company's directors, is in deep trouble. Things just don't seem to be going well–productivity is down and so is the bottom line. During our conversations, I try to uncover what the issues are. What I hear are statements like, "communication is poor...There's no trust or support...We're not bonding..."

When I stated the obvious–"So, you need some help with all those issues?" The CEO replied, "Yes, and it wouldn't hurt if we could learn to laugh together, as well."

That CEO was SO right! **It wouldn't hurt if you laugh together!** Think of the effects that come from laughing together–think of the bonding and camaraderie that follow naturally. Laughter can bring people together; bridge gaps; make people more comfortable...**The company that plays together certainly is more likely to stay together!**

Exercise:

Consider the question: *Are we laughing enough together at work?* When was the last time I shared a great laugh with my co-workers? How did I feel afterwards? Write your thoughts in your journal.

So, let's review

How would it be in our workplaces if we actually lived this Laughing Matters philosophy everyday?

- We would arise in the morning, energized and ready to face the day.
- We would be able to communicate simply and easily with co-workers and customers.
- We would smile while speaking on the phone or greeting others.
- The workday would fly by because we would feel happier and more fulfilled.
- At the end of the day, we would feel a great sense of accomplishment, and have the energy to go home and spend quality time with family and friends.

No, I'm not smoking those funny cigarettes and I'm not delusional–I'm just someone who loves what I do, knows that fun and laughing matters, and I'm having a great time persuading you to believe that your work can bring that same enjoyment to your life. How could anything be more fun than that?

Imagine the kind of responses I get when I talk to people about the importance of *lightening up with humor* in the workplace. Most people don't get it right away. They insist that work has to be about *working*; they can't see that the two concepts can co-exist–that work enhanced with fun can increase productivity exponentially. But now that *you* get it, I need your help. I need a team, deputized to help me prove that the concept of *fun in the workplace* really works!

I deputize you to go to work today and *live* the philosophy I've just shared. Be happy at work, love *something* about what you're doing and share it with everyone around you. Before you know it, you'll love more and more about what you're doing, until you really LOVE your workplace and your job. You can be a trendsetter and you *can* make a difference.

Let's eradicate terminal seriousness–at work *and* in your life–by starting to see the humor all around us–start right now! Are you in? GREAT! Congratulations–you're destined to make a huge difference and contribute to a great mission. Just imagine if this concept takes hold in your workplace, in your town, in your state, across the country...the possibilities are infinite!

Still not convinced of the *WHY*? Well, here's a final concept guaranteed to persuade you.

Paradigm: Employees first is the ultimate customer service.

Keeping employees happy is the most important component of customer service! What? Do I really mean that the first responsibility of corporate higher-ups is to their employees, not to their customers?? You mean, the customers who buy the product you sell should take a back seat to your company's employees? But that's *crazy*–you have to satisfy your customers or you won't have any business, *right? Wrong!!*

Let's analyze that.

Employees serve customers, so how employees are served, or treated, has an enormous impact on how they serve your clients. Once employees realize that management really believes they deserve good treatment, and once that good treatment materializes in the form of humor in the workplace, every employee will have the desire to pass that good feeling on to your customers. How your employees are served has a HUGE impact on how they serve your clients! Get it? Better service = more $$$$. Something to think about and something that can be encouraged and *taught* in the workplace, no matter which end of the ladder you're on!

Of course if you're on a ladder, you probably should know if you're on the top or the bottom and which direction you're going. It'll make it a whole lot easier to get there.

Your employees are your human assets *and* your most important customers!

Choose to Have Fun
Fun creates enjoyment
Enjoyment invites participation
Participation focuses attention
Attention expands awareness
Awareness promotes insight
Insight generates knowledge
Knowledge facilitates action
Action yields results

Oswald B. Swallow

Two

How Do We Really Know A Workplace Is Fun? or Does Your Workplace Have What It Takes? or What Makes A Great Workplace, Anyhow?

I couldn't decide again on just the right title. I'm a hopeless case about decisions. Well, maybe they won't care. :)

Fun has become an organizational strategy—a strategic weapon to achieve extraordinary results in areas of corporate life ranging from training sessions to meetings to hiring practices.

Dave Hemsath and Leslie Yerkes,
301 Ways to Have Fun at Work

How do we know when a workplace is fun and offers an environment that encourages our staff to want to come to work everyday? Does your workplace have what it takes? These are great questions. It all comes down to *what makes a particular workplace a more desirable place in which to work—rather than over at Joe's place down the street?* Why would someone actually prefer to work here rather than at Joe's and what's the payoff for you, the employer, CEO, manager, or staff member?

Well, maybe they serve better food at Joe's, or have a better break room...you might want to send a spy over to check it out.

Let's consider what it takes to have a workplace where people actually say..."It's fun here!" I mean, if I were to conduct a survey and ask you what is the most important thing about where you work, what would you say?

Yeah, like people would really be honest about answering these questions? Who are we kidding?

Exercise:

Take a moment to list what, to you, are the most important things about where you work.

Was the first item on the list *money*? Often, we think the first thought others have about what is important in the workplace is money. But that is not really the answer when one thinks about it more seriously. Let's try again. There really are things more important than a salary. In fact, in some cases, job applicants willingly accept an offer of less money in exchange for other things they consider much more important. For instance, how about ***loving what you do****?*

Think about the following list of criteria people might include when they think about rating their jobs. Give each some thought then follow along with the discussion that follows. The list order here is random–it is up to each person to identify his or her own order of priorities.

Depending on the emphasis an employer puts on each of the items on the list and how they are put in place determines the magnetism of a given workplace. Our discussion revolves around the results of a best case scenario; when a workplace has gotten it right, this is what happens.

As you proceed through the discussion, you will begin to accept a very important principle:

Paradigm: If people LOVE working for you, they will turn down other jobs that offer much more money.

The Criteria

Morale/Attitude

People actually enjoy–maybe even LOVE–going to work. They wake up, look forward to the day, come bounding into the office, and are excited to face new challenges. Sound unbelievable? Well, it's not. In a company where management believes in having a fun workplace and supports it, morale is high and the attitude is positive so this best case scenario is a reality.

Regrettably, this is a *magic key* that is missing in most workplaces and you'll see more discussion of that later.

When job hunting, how do you know that management supports an upbeat lighthearted workplace? It will be evident through the behavior of the employees, including those doing the interviewing. They will keep things very light and upbeat. Employees will relate to each other in a pleasant and friendly way and have a generous attitude towards one another. People will actually smile for no apparent reason. There will be a number of incentive and recognition programs in place so employees feel appreciated and rewarded.

Hmmm, appreciated and rewarded. Now there's a concept! Hello?

Exercise:

Make a list of what kind of morale-boosting incentive and recognition programs exist in your workplace (The kinds of programs that ensure that employees feel rewarded and appreciated). If your list is hard to see because it's not long enough, make a list of programs you think could make the workplace better and think about how to propose them to management.

Physical Environment

In the physical surroundings, it is evident that the environment works in a positive way. The walls are painted with bright colors and there is plenty of natural light. Employees have the freedom to decorate their offices to suit their personalities. Cubicles and offices are unique and reflect something about the person who occupies them. There may even be furniture that fits each person's taste rather than a single company style.

If company policy requires uniform furnishing, individuals can still make their own space more personal by decorating the walls and displaying some personal items. People might have toys or amusing items on their desks or walls (Artwork and vivid wall colors are great for livening up office space).

The overall working environment or public building space reflects lightheartedness with pastel colors and fun artwork. Break rooms promote positive ways for employees to recharge their batteries. Instead of standard vending machines or cafeteria style tables and chairs, there may be "stations"–a listening station with headphones and humorous or meditative CDs; a humor station with humorous books or cartoons; an art station with finger paints, crayons and coloring books or clay. There may even be a game station where staff members can play a quick game of checkers, or have an ongoing scrabble game or jigsaw puzzle going. Butcher block paper on the wall or a whiteboard can offer space for people to create a mural or cartoon, or play a quick game of "tic-tac-toe".

Now I know some bosses are probably panicking here and shaking in their shoes, worried people will wanna play all day... I hope they'll keep reading. I guess I just need to breathe and not get too anxious.

Break rooms will offer comfortable seating with sofas and comfortable chairs, with motivational books on a coffee table.

These are just a few ideas–the options are limitless! The important idea is that employees can rejuvenate themselves and forget work for 15 minutes or a half hour, then return to their desks with more energy, as opposed to going to the break room to smoke or fill up on junk food snacks.

Although, having Hershey kisses doesn't constitute junk food !? Some of us gotta have the chocolate!

Paradigm: If someone relaxes and distracts for awhile... they'll go back to work much more ready to focus and work... more productive.

Can you say "ka ching?"

Exercise:

Make a list of the physical aspects of your workplace that are conducive to good morale and what are some positive changes that can be made?

Flexibility

Flexibility is the ability to respond or adapt to change without suffering undue anxiety or fear. How do the management and employees of the company you're working at deal with expected and *un*expected changes? Can the staff consider lots of options? Is change embraced rather than perceived as a threat? Is there an ability to play with what's happening–to makes things fun? Do they focus on the present, rather than wallowing in the errors of the past? In the workplace we are looking for staff and management to learn to "reframe" negatives into positives and move forward in a pro-active way.

To be truly flexible and learn to embrace change takes practice and lots of it. The best way to practice is to interrupt an old habit and do something different from the way it is usually done.

Genie Z. Laborde wrote her classic book, ***Influencing With Integrity***, in the 1980s. She suggests some of the following ideas for practicing greater flexibility.

- If you drive to work, take a different route; or if you're close enough, ride your bike or walk, or–just for fun–skip part of the way!!
- Pretend that you have a different position at work and think of how you might handle a particular issue if the job were yours.
- Challenge yourself–do something you've never done before.
- In the middle of an argument or heated discussion, turn it into something positive–genuinely tell the other person that you think they are right after all. Ask them what they would like to do to solve a problem or create a change. If the other person is so shocked that they are speechless, walk them through creating a new set of options. You can then follow through or not.

Exercise:

Make a list of certain practices or work habits that you have in place. Reconsider each and list ways they could be made more flexible. Include both personal and work-related habits.

Innovation and Creativity

There is a feeling of innovation and creative spirit within the organization. People feel inspired by the physical environment and by their co-workers. For example, I live in Austin, Texas. We have a very well-known, successful advertising agency in town. The employees can create their own individual office motif by including a chaise lounge or high stools and a counter instead of a traditional desk, or whatever they might think of. There are certain parts of the building devoted to their different accounts. For example, there is an airline section for one of their advertisers which includes a display of a plane hanging from the ceiling and airline memorabilia. This kind of environment promotes a sense of humor and play so that people are inspired and more creative.

When innovation and creativity are encouraged by management, staff can experience receptivity of their ideas. Rather than feeling shut down or "wrong" about their input, ideas are welcome. There is permission to share ideas and for people's sharing to be welcomed. Ideas are processed and considered and, even though they can't all be accepted, ideas are heard and considered.

Imagine… someone actually considers your ideas! Boy, I hope they like mine.

In this creative environment, everyone is focused on positive outcome (rather than failure). People approach new ideas and new projects with an attitude of spontaneity and joy.

Creativity abounds!

Exercise:

Think about and write down ways to create opportunities for creativity and innovation and then increase the list by 50%!.

Reputation

A company's reputation, or how it is thought of by the outside world, is a combination of the image the company promotes or advertises, and how the community-at-large perceives it. This is a result of articles and word-of-mouth and information supplied by its employees. How is your company seen by the outside world. Have you heard people talking about it?

(yeah, well maybe they wish they hadn't)

If it is a large, well-known company, you might have lunch where some of the employees are known to eat and just eavesdrop. What do you hear? How do the employees seem to feel about it? To meet the criteria of our best-case scenario, you should hear things like: the company is viewed by the employees and people in the community as a fun place to work; employees like being at work and they have permission to be light-hearted with freedom to be spontaneous and have fun.

Regrettably, many companies that have done surveys to measure employee satisfaction have found that over 50% of the employees surveyed would leave their jobs in a heartbeat and go elsewhere–even for less money–if they were certain a job was available. Why? Most said, simply, they were miserable at work. Too many employees feel unappreciated and overworked; executives often consider the company to be in a constant state of crisis. And, guess what?

These people live in the community and talk about the company and how they feel about it. It becomes known that misery is the order-of-the-day. Now, back to our eavesdropping lunch–overhearing such a scenario, who will be anxious to apply for a job there? In a tough economy, existing employees may stay put, but when the job market opens up, good employees will bail out and such companies will experience employee shortages and really find themselves in crisis.

So, what are the *bad* companies doing to lighten up the workplace–even when they are aware of their negative reputations? Obviously, not enough–*They* have never been to HumorU, (a humble company, dedicated to fun and enlivening workplaces–www.humoru.com)

A mercenary plug here–AND an opportunity to learn more about humor … and me, of course!

or tried to turn their company's attitude problem on its ear, figuratively speaking. So, their reputation continues to decline and Wall Street will likely reflect their flaws over time. They will NEVER make it onto a list of the top 100 fun places to work.

Will you?

The moral of this scenario is: *it is common knowledge that when a company is a great, fun place to work, applications pile in and these companies have the best applicants to choose from. Once hired, employees want to stay and dedicate themselves, working harder than ever to have their company succeed.*

Exercise:

Do a survey. Find out what people are saying about your company. Do you agree with what you hear? Does it accurately represent your company's personality—does what you hear reflect the reputation of your company in an accurate way? Give it some thought. Is it time for action?

Vision and Mission Statement

What is your company's vision? Does it have a mission statement? Does either include the words *fun* and *joy*? Many companies now embrace this concept enough to include it in all of their company literature. They often have a FUN committee in place to enhance the positive atmosphere and to achieve the mission of FUN.

What a concept!

Is this too short and simple a criteria? Maybe they'll think I don't know anything about creating mission or visions. I mean I know companies spend months coming up with these things.... But don't they know it's really simple?

Exercise:

Write your NEW company mission and vision statement. Make sure that it inspires you. And, if you're brave enough, you might want to submit them to your CEO for consideration.

Playfulness of the Culture

Although many of the criteria we've laid out speak to playfulness, generally there are a few other important points to make here. In a light-hearted culture, people naturally collaborate. They seek each other out, they like being together, and they work well together. Competition is of a healthy sort and everyone is encouraged to be their best. Employees admire each other's work and actually enjoy being on projects together. Humor is encouraged.

For example, the great ad agency we mentioned earlier needs their staff to be very creative, so playfulness abounds. In their building, there is a basketball hoop in the rotunda and people play in the middle of the day. There are games and opportunities to play throughout the building. Management hosts events to foster camaraderie which informally stimulates team building–a nice by-product. This is the perfect picture of wise leadership and a successful company–they provide a positive atmosphere and the staff responds by giving their best.

A playful culture holds many celebrations for everyday events–they celebrate employee recognition, they have contests for fun, for holidays, and for new concept ideas. The positive attitude spreads beyond the workplace and includes family members and the community at large. Everyone knows about the company's activities. And, isn't that the point? Everyone knows and everyone wants to be a part of it.

Hello .. like isn't this the crux of this whole treatise?

Exercise:

Okay, this is the focal point of the whole book. Make a list of how playful your company is. What kinds of fun things are happening and what kinds of things does your company celebrate? Check it twice and make it longer.

Paradigm: Happy employees are more creative, more motivated, and work more cooperatively as team members. And most important—they help you strive toward your company's mission.

More Criteria:

Let's think about some other criteria that might not be as readily apparent or expected in creating a fun workplace. Let's go with the premise that a company or organization is, basically, a collection of individuals. Bear that in mind during this discussion. By the way, we identified these criteria through the work of a good friend and incredibly competent consultant, Paul Schumann of Glocal Vantage, Inc. (http://www.glocalvantage.com) Paul put together an extensive survey and administered it to a large group of people to find out what they considered to be important in a workplace. He added the following criteria to our list for great companies.

Self-Actualization

Self-actualization is defined as the inner drive toward experiencing and expressing the totality of one's being through spiritual, psychological, physical, and mental exercises which enhance the development of one's maximum potential. **People are encouraged to grow and be themselves.**

Confidence

Confidence is a realistic and objective belief that one has the skills to achieve in the world of work and to feel that those skills are a positive contribution. **Pats on the back help a lot.**

Synergy

Synergy is experiencing the relationships of persons within a group to be harmonious and energized so that the outcome of the group far surpasses its predicted ability based on the total abilities of its individual members. **People work together well and produce greater results than they could alone.**

Communication

Communication refers to the effective and efficient transmission and flow of ideas and factual data within and between persons, departments and divisions of an organization. **People actually talk and laugh together.**

Oh my!

Human Dignity

Human dignity refers to consciousness of the basic right of every human being to have respect and to have his/her basic needs met that will allow him/her the opportunity to develop his/her potential. **How will people feel cared about and respected?**

Collaboration

Collaboration is the ability of an organizational leader to cooperate interdependently with all levels of management, ensuring full and appropriate delegation of responsibility. **Everyone's input is important.**

People Centered

When an organization is "people centered", it is concerned with its employees. This is in opposition to being driven merely by money, profit, product development, etc. It indicates a step towards caring and compassion. It delivers top-rate customer service and usually begins by respecting it's #1 customers–it's employees. A company that is FUN is much more likely to be people centered. And, if you ask the employees, they will be able to identify this as a criteria for employment.

Think about what your company calls the department that is in charge of the people. Is it the H.R. Dept? Or is it the People Dept? Wal-mart has a People Department and so do many other companies now.

Exercise:

Review these last seven criteria and rate their presence or absence at your company. Journal the changes and additions you would like to make.

"Most helpful humor involves the good-natured contemplation of life's incongruities. One can respond either with anger and violence or with humor. Therefore, we must conclude that humor is more than the ability to see our pretensions, contradictions and deceits. It is the ability to perceive these paradoxes from a position of emotional distance ... A highly effective sense of humor can help us view the present annoyance in a similar manner to the way we view it sometime in the future."

Dr. Laurence J. Peter

"It dawned on me then that as long as I could laugh, I was safe from the world; and I have learned since that laughter keeps me safe from myself, too. All of us have schnozzles—are ridiculous in one way or another, if not in our faces, then in our characters, minds or habits. When we admit our schnozzles, instead of defending them, we begin to laugh, and the world laughs with us."

Jimmy Durante

THREE

It's All About Perspective

What's the best way to revolutionize the workplace? Forget restructuring and re-engineering. Have a little fun!
Matt Weinstein, Managing To Have Fun

Keep your eyes and ears open for the natural things you see and hear all the time and CHOOSE to look at them with a bit of irony or from another perspective. You can always find one.

Exercise:

Stand by your window and look outside. Look for about 30 seconds and notice everything you can; take it all in and see what brings a smile to your face. Now, turn around, with your back to the window, spread your legs apart, bend over, way down, like you're going to touch the floor, and look back out through the window by looking through your legs. Do you see things differently? This is obviously a different perspective, and it's kind of fun. Write down what you saw.

You know the saying about looking at the world through rose-colored glasses? You can! You can choose to look at everything differently. You can see something as black and white or in "Technicolor!"

So, let's take this a step further…into the work environment. How can you alter your perspective and perception at work? How can you see or hear things differently? The answer lies in being more innovative, creative and different. Here are some ideas.

1. During your next meeting, have everyone wear a clown nose or wig or funny glasses or the "loudest" shirt they can find. Believe me, the meeting will look and sound very different than it normally would.
2. Break your employees up into groups of 5 during a team-building event. Give each group a "goody bag"– i.e.: cotton balls, paper clips, yarn, a coffee mug and about 8 or 10 other items. Make sure every group has exactly the same items. Now, ask each group to "build" a useful thing to present to the rest of the groups. You'll notice that every group's construction will be different. Each group will come up with something unique based on the perspective of the particular people in the group.
3. On a Friday afternoon, close your doors and take the entire staff to a new movie that is debuting that day. (Send someone down early to buy tickets to insure you'll all be able to get in.) Announce it as a surprise. Take them down on buses. How do you think that would affect the team perspective? (You know, the work really can wait a couple of hours. Nothing terrible will happen.)

Author's Note

I attended a conference recently called "The Heart of Happiness". There were many speakers, including a highly respected American Buddhist practitioner. His presentation was about "Lightening up and *En*lightening Up". Of course, I had to check out his session. I've always thought that a Buddhist practitioner would be a serious, sage-like individual with flowing robes. Well, I felt pretty silly when I realized that he looked just like you or me–a regular guy wearing slacks and a shirt with rolled-up sleeves. He sat on a stool on stage and proceeded to share with us the early beginnings of the Buddha and, what he referred to as, "crazy wisdom". He likened spirituality to lightening up and said they are part of the same path. He also said that, **"...humor breaks through the difficulty of facing life and situations."** And he finished with "Spirituality is pure joy!" Then he closed with a Buddhist joke:

How many Buddhists does it take to change a light bulb? It takes 10–one to change the bulb and 9 to "share the experience."

Moral of the story: It doesn't take much to change our perspective. It takes just playing with what you see and hearing and finding a different fun interpretation. It takes tapping into the sense of "joy" and spirit. Once you get the hang of it, it's pretty easy.

Exercise:

Here's another way to use a change in perspective. Think of a problem you're having right now—maybe one that you've been trying to solve for awhile. Think about it and then ask yourself, "How would a 5 year old deal with this?" What about an 85-year old? Your favorite comedian? Your dog or cat? Did you come up with some new ideas about solving your problem? Journal your ideas.

Exercise:

Do something this week to change your perspective at work. What will you do to teach others so that they can change their perspectives, too?

Sometimes people ask me what it takes to develop a better sense of humor. I say, "not much." That's the truth. All you need to do is pump up your perspective a bit. Look for things all around you. You know how Leno and Letterman make fun of headlines, politics, and unusual, everyday stuff? That's really what it's all about.

Author's note

Now I am going to 'tell one on myself.' People who know me well have noticed from time to time, that I tend to be more of a "cup half-empty" than a "cup half-full" kind of person. If there's a negative side, I'll sometimes dwell there a bit longer than necessary.

Now that's an understatement. I've actually been known to move in and live there... for months ... yep, just me and my cats, living there, furrballs and all.

Do I like that about myself? Well, not especially, and I have come to the conclusion that it's probably "hard-wired" into my personality. The good news, though, is that, over the years, I've learned to compensate for and manage it.

Also, my friends know that I'm not a comedian–I couldn't remember the punch line to a joke if my life depended on it–Really! Does that mean I'm not funny? Absolutely not. I can be hilarious. I think in a way that looks at situations in all different ways. I put on my "perspective glasses" and I look at things and issues from all sides. I do this all the time and I surprise myself (and others) with how I relate to the world. I also mentally catalog examples that I can share.

Let me share one with you here. I recently pulled up to a drive-through ATM machine to withdraw some cash. I pushed all the appropriate numbers and buttons and, while waiting for my cash, I noticed that the machine panel contained, what I assume was, a translation in Braille. Think about it–a drive-through, with Braille.

We could really be in trouble here.

The next day I went into a restaurant and there was a big sign that said, "Braille menus available upon request."

Of course we can figure out the rationale behind both of these...you know, someone else is with the visually-impaired person, yada, yada, yada. However, I chose to look at the humorous side. It gave me a few chuckles and something to write and speak about. In fact, I recently related this story to a large audience. A man, who *was* visually-impaired came up to me afterwards–he thought it was hilarious and gave me some examples of his own to add to my list.

There are circumstances like that all around you–just be open to it when you see it.

Of course, you have to go through life with your eyes open...like looking at everything around you . And, having a warped sense of humor helps a lot too.

Exercise:

Keep a list of what you see now that you likely wouldn't have noticed before. Take pictures to share it with others. Happy Looking!!

"I have a 'carpe diem' mug and, truthfully, at six in the morning the words do not make me want to seize the day. They make me want to slap a dead poet!"

Joanne Sherman

FOUR

The Big Challenges: Change and Stress

If you can find humor in anything, you can survive it.
Bill Cosby

In spite of whatever happens at work or in your personal life, always remember that **how you feel is entirely up to you. You create it! You can choose humor and light-heartedness just as easily as misery!**

Let's discuss the how(s) and why(s) of humor as a healing agent. It's not really rocket science, after all. Here's the gist of it.

- You figure out what makes you laugh or feel good
- You do it
- You laugh and lighten up!!

It's really very simple.

As human beings, it's pretty interesting what we do about life. We have a tendency to make everything hard, serious, dramatic. We love to complain and find fault. Our conversations are often, "I don't wanna, I can't, It's too hard, blah, blah, blah and blah!" What do you think happens to us as a result of our constant whining and complaining and negative thinking?

Well for starters, do we get that people are running the other way?

Hello? Well, amazingly that complaining costs us big time, in many, many ways. It costs us our happiness, our connection with other people, our power, our emotional health, our physical well-being. We often become miserable around others and then they don't want to be around us. They start avoiding us, walking the other way when they see us coming. We don't get invited out to lunch or other events. We eventually don't even like being with ourselves.

Do you get it? It's like having the plague.

Magnets

Imagine an alternative to what we described above. What if we were happy? What if we laughed a lot and had an upbeat attitude? How would people feel about being around us then? Well, they would come towards us; they would love to hang out with us because we make them laugh; we'd get invited to parties and events; they would invite us home to meet their gorgeous sisters or brothers or parents or cousins; everyone would gravitate to us just like they want us as family. The match-making and inclusion techniques would be amazing. Wow! We would be like **magnets**–attracting everything we want.

What would that be like for us? First, we'd be happier and we would actually like being in our own company, in addition to others wanting to be in our company. We'd be healthier because laughter and well-being contribute to physical health. We'd have lots of friends to do things with. We'd probably even land the great job we set our sights on.

Whew - I hope they don't think I'm promising these things! I have really no clue whether these things will happen or not, but hey, I'm the one writing it and it sounds good to me!

I've spoofed and simplified it, but you get the picture. The truth is, people *like* to be around happy people.

Well most people do, unless they're the unhappy ones who like the company of misery, And we all know that there are LOTS of those around.

So, to sum it all up, yes–sometimes life hands us lemons (change, stress, pimples); so, do we make the proverbial lemonade, or do we suck on sour lemons? To put it another way, we can be **magnets** just holding up papers on a refrigerator, or we can be **magnetic** and attract amazing things to us. Which would you rather be? Be miserable and attract misery, or be happy and attract happiness and **opportunity**? If you're unemployed, take it as an opportunity to see what's next for you in your life and go for it. Don't let discouragement and fear paralyze you. Instead, let the excitement of new possibilities activate you; be an opportunist and attract opportunity.

They're probably wondering what this whole "woo woo" pep talk has to do with change and stress. Guess I should move on to it before they start rolling their eyes or yawning.

There are two major issues that can conflict with the ability to attract life and roll with the punches and recognize opportunity when you see it. Those issues are **change and stress**. We all face them and it behooves us to learn to gain mastery over them. Let's examine them one at a time. Even though this chapter addresses more serious issues, I promise we'll have some fun and great ideas for resolving issues at the end of it.

"I–I hardly know, sir, just at present." Alice replied rather shyly. "At least I know who I was when I got up this morning, but I think I must have been changed several times since then."

Lewis Carroll, Alice in Wonderland

"It's not so much that we're afraid of change or so in love with the old ways, but it's that place in between that we fear… it's like being between trapezes. It's Linus when his blanket is in the dryer: There's nothing to hold on to."

Marilyn Ferguson

Change

Consider this: You are here–**X**–this spot and this moment is exactly where you are now; not tomorrow and not yesterday! Maybe you'd like to be someplace else right now in your life; or maybe you're happy and content with this moment. But, *in this moment you are.* A corollary of this is that you're exactly where you are meant to be and you're exactly where everything that has happened thus far in your life has brought you–to this very moment in time.

In other words: 1) Wherever you go, there you are; and 2) sometimes you need to go where you're being taken.

The one absolute thing we do know about work and life is that CHANGE HAPPENS! *Change is certain–blink your eyes and when you open them, things will be different than they were a moment ago–they will have changed.*

Have you ever signed on to work someplace only to find out that all the reasons you wanted to work there changed in what seemed only days after you joined the company?

Yeah, like way too many times I bet.

Have you ever felt like you knew exactly what was expected of you; you knew you were performing at your peak, only to find out the job description was changed without your knowing it? All of a sudden, you felt like a bull in a china shop; totally out of place and you didn't know which way was up or where to turn?

Maybe you're just directionally challenged, like me.

To ignore change is like having the proverbial elephant in the middle of the living room with no one talking about it. (By the way, how do you eat an elephant? One bite at a time!!!!!)

HOW DO YOU DEAL WITH CHANGE?
ONE bite AT A TIME!!!

Oh gosh, I might be in trouble with this one. I know elephants are endangered. I'm not trying to be disrespectful here… just want to make a point. What if I offend them? Will they stop reading. It's just the best way I know how to make this point.

Maybe you even say a little prayer, like one of these:

1. Grant me the serenity to accept the things I cannot change, the courage to change the things I cannot accept, and the wisdom to hide the bodies of those people I had to kill today 'cause they really made me mad! Or…
2. Help me to be careful of the toes I step on today, as they may be connected to the butt that I might have to kiss tomorrow.

But just in case neither of those prayers works, I guess we better think about how to really deal with change.

Uh oh. Now I have to try and come up with something concrete. Time to think!

So, where do we start? Begin by asking yourself, "What bothers me the most about change?"

Often the answer has something to do with feeling out of control. What else? Think harder. Can you think of a time that change produced a positive outcome and maybe was even fun? If you can find an answer to that question, it will be easier to handle what's changing now. Continuing the inquiry, especially if you *can't* think of a past change experience that was positive, ask yourself if you can get used to the change anyway. In other words, will you be able to tolerate some change and eventually adapt to it? If you think you will be able to adapt, then hang in there and work with it. If you really don't think you can deal with it or accept it, then maybe it's time to move on.

Once you've decided to stay and face a change, come from the position of a different perspective. Remember, we looked at this in Chapter three. Examine all the changes being made and ask yourself the questions: How would a 5-year-old handle this? How would an 85-year-old, my cat, my dog, or my favorite comedian handle it?

Answering these questions may give you a whole new insight into dealing with whatever scary change is lurking out there. These questions get you outside of yourself to a place where you're thinking outside of your *normal* box; you can see it looking from the outside in–a totally different perspective!

Exercise:

Journal about a time when you handled change well and another time when you totally botched it and what you learned from both of these experiences.

Surrender

After the inquiry, begin to face the change(s) head on, from the perspective of the Zen masters. In the Zen tradition, you come to learn that there is the dichotomy of struggle vs. surrender. You can struggle or suffer or you can go with the flow–it's that simple. Let's examine a couple of examples of that dichotomy.

- Remember the childhood tune, *Row, row, row your boat–gently down the stream; merrily, merrily, merrily, merrily, life is but a dream.* It says "down" the stream; in other words, go with the flow–not "up" the stream, where you have to fight against the oncoming current. Struggle or surrender?

In the same way, *change* is much more difficult when you resist. So, surrender–it's the better choice!

- How about this one: "Ride the horse in the direction it's going." [Werner Erhard] You can go with the horse in the same direction as the rest of the horses, or you can go against them. Which is more likely to keep you on your horse and get you where you might be going, instead of fighting the horse and likely ending up in the mud in the middle of nowhere?

Yuck!

Struggle or surrender? Surrender... the better choice!

- And, finally, this one: "You don't have to attend every fight you're invited to." You can choose to fight every battle and suffer and struggle, or you can choose to sit some out."

Personally, I prefer sitting to fighting any day… takes much less energy and I hate blood and guts.

Struggle or Surrender? Surrender … definitely, the better choice!

Let's turn to an old Chinese parable to distinguish some points about change:

There was once an old farmer who had a mare. One day the mare broke through a fence and ran away.

"Now you have no horse to pull your plow at planting time." The neighbors said, "What bad luck this is."

"Good luck, bad luck," the farmer replied. "Who knows?"

The next week, the mare returned bringing with her two wild stallions.

"With three horses you are now a rich man," the neighbors said. "What good fortune this is."

"Good fortune, bad fortune." The farmer replied. "Who knows?"

That afternoon the farmer's only son tried to tame one of the stallions, but he was thrown and broke his leg.

"Now you have no one to help with the planting," the neighbors said. "What bad luck this is."

"Bad luck, good luck," the farmer replied. "Who knows?"

The next day, the Emperor's soldiers rode into town and conscripted the eldest son of every family, but the farmer's son was left behind because of his broken leg.

"Your son is the only male in the province who has not been taken from his family," the neighbors said. "What good fortune this is..."

Moral: What often seems to be the most horrible situation can usher in *wonderful* opportunities or outcomes.

Of course, there's the opposite, like when bad situations really are bad, but we won't go there now. Remember, Ann, keep it light and upbeat!.

So, one moment, something is one way and then the next moment, it isn't. Change can be huge, like a disaster or tragedy (9/11 or Columbine). Change can be a major negative or unexpected, like divorce, business failure, car accident. Or, it can be minor like change of location, being late, finding an error in your manuscript. Or, change can be irritating like lost luggage, splattered ketchup on your clothes, losing your keys...

The only thing you can count on is that change happens…wham! Just like that. So, you might as well accept that change will always be present. You can allow it to make you miserable or–here's another thought–how about if you embrace change as a GIFT? So much good can come from change that it truly *is* a gift.

Enough touchy feely stuff or they'll throw this book in the board room garbage can. Time to shift gears.

That which does not kill me, makes me stronger!

Friedrich Neitzshe

Exercise:

Think of a time when something changed and the outcome proved amazingly better than you could have imagined. How about another time? List the "gifts" that change has brought.

We all know that change creates stress (probably related to the struggle/surrender dichotomy). In the Chinese tradition, stress has two symbols–one for crisis and one for opportunity. As you consider change, does it create for you a crisis or an opportunity? How easy it is to forget that each one of us has the choice to create our reaction–crisis or opportunity, even though we might have NO control over the changes.

Like, hello, we HAVE no control over change...that's what makes it change. It just happens, without control. Isn't that the point of this conversation?

Stress

What is stress? Webster's dictionary defines stress as:

1. A force that tends to strain or deform. 2. Mental, emotional, or physical tension, strain, or distress.

The Official Scrabble Player Dictionary (a more significant literary guide to me and my personal favorite) defines it as:

1. To place emphasis on

So things that stress us out are things that we put emphasis on. Here's the way I see it - **Stuff happens**. Things, out of our control and even in our control, happen all around us, all the time. Whether it is in the arena of work, relationships, finances, health, traffic, etc....stuff happens. STRESS is the meaning we give it. (More about that as we move on.)

I can create stress for you in a heartbeat. Try this:

Go to your immediate boss as quickly as you can. Tell him/her the following:

- How much you weigh
- How you really feel about your salary
- Your political affiliation
- How you really feel about your job
- How you really feel about your spouse/significant other or how you feel about not having one
- What you would rather be doing than being at work in this moment.

Now, you might have a great relationship with your boss, but that doesn't mean you'd be so bold as to really share these statements. In fact, you'd probably be feeling quite uncomfortable about sharing them. This exercise COULD stress you out. But, you don't have to let it. And, you can choose not to do it.

Or, you could do it, which would be really pretty stupid...but perhaps a "bonding" experience or...a way out the door.

Exercise:

Write your reactions to the following questions in your journal: How did you feel about the suggestion above? Did you talk to your boss? Did you read it and call me a few indecent names? Did you see how quickly you could get "stressed out"?

A couple of major premises.

1. Stress is bad for you! You are stressed... only because you allow yourself to be stressed!
2. Humor is good for you

I'm going to be serious for a moment and share some information about how stress affects our physical health. Some of the physical and psychological symptoms of stress include:

- headaches & fatigue
- increased consumption of alcohol, nicotine, coffee or drugs
- sleep disturbances
- moodiness or irritability
- depression
- feelings of helplessness, hopelessness or overwhelm
- feeling of being out-of-control of self
- communication difficulties

If these symptoms are showing up in your employees, in you or just generally at work...how is that contributing to performance on the job? How is that contributing to people's sense of purpose and commitment and loyalty to their job? And, if they are not committed to performing/producing on the job, **what is that costing your company?**

I definitely need my bullhorn here. Yes... this is the point... STRESS is costing you a lot of money!

How, you say? It detracts from the bottom line through health and mental health expenses, insurance claims, workman's comp. claims, absenteeism, violence, recruitment and replacement costs and low morale.

Can you hear the dollars and cents falling out of the bank balance here?

Are you scraping the bottom of the money barrel?

Here are a few of my outrageous estimates on the cost of stress:

I don't really know where these figures came from, so I better just paraphrase here. Oops.

- It is estimated that stress costs billions of dollars annually in sub-par performance, lateness and insurance claims.
- The majority of all medical office visits are stress-related–high blood pressure, chronic pain, anxiety, substance abuse, marital/family problems.
- Employee interviews indicate that nearly half of American workers considered quitting their jobs because of excessive stress. One-third of the workers expected stress to lead to eventual burnout if they don't leave.

So, what is *your* company doing to reduce stress in the workplace? There are, of course, the traditional stress management techniques–deep breathing, meditation, and exercise. They certainly work, for some. But what about laughter or fun ways to reduce your stress?

Actually, what about sleep?

In looking at the year 2003, with a downturn in the economy, layoffs and retention aren't much of an issue because people have few jobs they can leave for. But, they are definitely miserable and have stress staying in the jobs they have. Companies today are under constant pressure to produce and meet their goals. And just like a pressure cooker, if there isn't a way to relieve the "steam" (read that "stress") then it can explode. Not literally of course, but in terms of employees being unable to handle the pressure and then quitting or getting sick. There has to be a release valve for all that pressure *and laughter is a very cost-effective solution.* If fast, fast, fast, relief is what you're after, then laughter really *is* the best medicine!

Our cave-dwelling ancestors were stressed by actual life-threatening situations

---

Like being eaten by woolly mammoths.

But, times have changed. It is estimated that 72% of American workers experience frequent stress-related physical or mental conditions everyday. There are many different signs that point to ***the need for lightening up the workplace***, especially today with mergers, downsizing, little to no ethics, companies closing. Job security is almost nonexistent. Experts believe the hidden effects of stress are costing American firms uncalculated billions of dollars each year in lost productivity, absenteeism, and health-care expenses. Because the need is not always obvious, the most common signs suggesting it's time for an injection of humor are:

- Increase in people being fired or laid off
- Increase in sick time taken for depression
- Increased use of employee assistance programs
- Increase in job turnover
- Increase in job insecurity complaints

Stress doesn't exist in the outside world without it first existing in your head. **Getting a new perspective is what humor is all about**. By directing your comic vision inward, you can change your perceptions of a stressful situation and create some momentary calm. **It's virtually impossible to laugh and feel bad at the same time**. Try it! If you're caught in a situation you can't escape or change (a traffic jam, for example), then humor may be the healthiest form of temporary stress release possible.

In my popular workshop, "How to Lighten Up and Feel Good for the Rest of Your Life", I share the five secrets of what it takes. **"You can't feel bad and good at the same time"** is the #1 secret.

Humor works by someone stepping back from a situation and playing up its absurdities (remember the Perspective chapter?) The same kind of objective observation makes the tale of your disastrous business trip seem funny–**after** you get safely home. For stress busting**, the trick is to find ways to laugh at the situation while it's happening.** That's what people are doing when you see them smiling or laughing to themselves, as though there's no one else around ... they are amusing themselves inwardly rather than allowing themselves to be consumed by the stress of the situation. The major advantage of directing humor inward is that you only have to amuse yourself. You don't have to worry if anyone else will get it. It's your stress, and you can reduce it by thinking about things you find humorous. Even if you don't consider yourself much of a comedian, here are a few simple techniques you can use(I learned many of these from my colleague, Terrill Fischer):

- **Pick a safe subject**: Making fun of your own mistakes can save face in an embarrassing situation–you'll have people laughing with you, rather than at you. Inanimate sources of frustration, like parking spaces, computers and copying machines, are also safe objects of humor. You can't make fun of the executives, but it is perfectly all right to make fun of the executive parking spaces.
- **The Seinfeld maneuver**: How would your favorite Seinfeld character or cartoon character react to the situation? Just imagining what would happen can give you a laugh, making the situation less annoying. You can even pretend you're the star of a TV drama, and this stressful episode is tonight's plot.

I won't play this game though if George and Kramer aren't in the scenes with me.

- **Exaggerate your dilemma; consciously overstate your problem**: Blow it completely out of proportion and into absurdity–into a comedy routine. If you can't change your physical setting, change your mental one, with humor, by answering your own "what-ifs" with humorous solutions. In that long line of traffic, don't say "This traffic is killing me; I hate this." Ask: "What if…this traffic never gets moving? I have to live in my car? The woman/guy in the car in front of me is incredibly gorgeous and wants to move into my car with me?"

  This maneuver helps take the edge off the situation, redirects your tension and helps you see things as not so impossible after all.

Your running commentary, however, is probably best kept to yourself. Others might not understand or might have the people in white coats come and take you away.

- **Lay it on the line:** Sometimes just telling the truth or pointing out the obvious can get a laugh. People are accustomed to exaggeration and truth bending (too many TV commercials, perhaps), so plain speaking can come as a refreshing break. I've been known to put everyone in stitches by simply replying to a question with "Gee, I don't know" or "I'm clueless." This kind of humor is a way of fighting stress by accepting our shortcomings.

Not that I really have any shortcomings.
I'm just pretending to be humble.

- **Clip a cartoon**: Keep a file of jokes and cartoons that make you laugh. Paste a few up where you're likely to need them–at work, on the refrigerator, at home on your bathroom mirror, wherever. The comic relief provided by the cartoons eases some of the stress caused by the issues represented in the cartoons.

So, the choice is yours. When the stress bug bites you–what will you do? Will you succumb to it, let it build up pressure like a pressure cooker? Or, will you, instead, choose to "lighten up?" Let's see–hmm, **feel bad or feel good**?–it's a tough choice–but, I'll put my money on feeling good! What about you???

I mean "ugh", why would anyone want
to feel bad? Well, maybe they're
masochists. But let's not go there.

For businesses and employees, dealing with stress is rooted in taking numerous small fun steps to alleviate it. The key to making humor work for any company is to help employees improve their own humor-coping skills. Here are some of my recommended STRESS RELEASE or "LIGHTEN UP" EXERCISES.

Downloading your stress

This is one of my favorite activities for stress reduction.

1. Prior to beginning the process, each person thinks of a stressful event they've experienced within the past couple of days

2. Choose a partner to "download" your stress to
3. One person agrees to go first
4. The person going first will talk and the other will listen (without talking)
5. The person talking will have one minute (60 seconds) to talk very quickly and in an animated fashion about the stressful event they experienced. At the end of 60 seconds, they will switch. If they're worried about disclosing the nature of their stress, they can "download" it in gibberish using unintelligible language or sounds or by saying "blah, blah, blah…"

Even if you use real words, they probably just hear blah, blah anyhow. Do you think they really listen? I don't think so!

---

6. After both have "downloaded" their stress, they'll talk about how they started to lighten up as a result of exaggerating and talking fast. The likelihood is that they will feel better as a result of the exercise. They might even be laughing.

Getting rid of perfectionism

Perfectionism places totally unnecessary expectations on an individual. People have a sense that if they don't perform a task "perfectly" that "something bad will happen"

Like the ceiling will cave in or the world will come to an end…

To prove them false, here's a fun exercise:

1. Fold a piece of paper in half and hold it in the hand you do not write with.
2. Take a crayon and hold it in the hand you do write with.
3. Place the paper against your forehead

4. Place the crayon against the paper and write the name of the most important person in your life. Write it in cursive – trying of course, to do it as ***perfectly*** as possible.
5. When finished, take the paper down and look at it–it will produce roaring laughter AND it will not be perfect AND, nothing bad will have happened as a result of it not being perfect.

Brain dump

This is great for ridding yourself of any remaining annoyances.

1. Start with a blank piece of paper
2. On the paper, write, draw or scribble down everything and anything that is bothering you–work that isn't done, personal issues (like finances, relationships, etc), stuff that's just on your mind. DUMP it all on the paper, using crayons–list things, draw stick figures or symbols–whatever works. The important thing is to get it all down.
3. Once completed, take the paper, fold it up into a paper airplane and sail it into the garbage can–thus ridding yourself of all your stress. If your stress is really making you angry you could even burn your paper in a empty trash can, just make sure you don't burn down your office.

Better have your fire extinguisher close by.

After all of the above exercises are done–go out to the playground, go for a swim or a walk, go to the zoo, go shopping, go to a movie, play a game or do something that will be fun for the rest of the day. I guarantee you that without stress for even part of one day, you will return to your workplace very refreshed and highly productive.

Or you actually could decide to never return–hope your boss won't blame me. Sorry!

Remember I said earlier that stress is merely a REACTION–your reaction to something going on around you. So, if you can choose to react to it–you can also choose NOT to react to it. Instead you can choose to find ways to laugh and have fun which in turn stimulates blood flow, strengthens your immune system, and reduces levels of hormones that create stress; all of which could have positive effects on your creativity and productivity.

Stress and Change Solutions:
"Conscious Choosing" and Humor

In essence, there's one major way to handle any of these situations. It's called CHOOSING.. Remember the principle I shared earlier, under my 5 Secrets of how to Lighten Up and Feel Good for the Rest of Your Life? It's the Number One principle: "You can't feel bad and good at the same time?" It's true. You can feel bad or you can feel good–you choose. No one else can choose for you. Ever have someone try to get you to feel good when you didn't want to? It doesn't work.

Doesn't work for me. When I want to feel bad, I do and nobody can stop me. They shouldn't even try.

No matter what the circumstance, it's up to you. What power and freedom there is to know that. All you have to do, minute by minute is choose. I think I'll call this **"conscious choosing."** I mean, there's being in the "conscious moment" and there's "conscious playing." Now there's conscious "choosing."

Remember, stress is only a reaction–how you react to a situation or a circumstance. Since it's your reaction, you're the only one who can do anything about it.

Although they probably think that someone else should be able to do something about it.

So, choose humor. I know it sometimes is a difficult thing to do. I'll continue striving to convince you of how important it is, especially as it relates to the hard areas of change and stress at work:

- Humor ENERGIZES your workforce. When people are happy, they smile and laugh and their attitude becomes contagious to all around them. Humor builds "espirit de corps."
- Humor CHANGES PERSPECTIVE at work. Instead of seeing the pot as half empty, humor helps you see it as half full.

If only we'd stop trying to be happy we could have a pretty good time.
Edith Wharton

- Humor creates greater SAFETY for looking at the problems and looking at FEELINGS.

Feelings at work, oh my! That'll get a couple of raised eyebrows.

- Humor is the cement/the bonding material that connects people at work.

Takes the words "stuck on you" to a whole different level.

The shortest distance between two people is a laugh!

Victor Borge

- Humor makes it easier to talk about difficult issues.

I try to take one day at a time, but sometimes several days attack me at once.

Jennifer Unlimited

Author's note

Case in point: Several years ago, I was called in to offer a "playshop"–a workshop focusing on relieving the stress for all the employees who were being laid off because their plant was shutting down. They had been involved in a very intense project for many years; but the switch got pulled and the project was cancelled. So, not only were they all out of a job, but the project they were passionate about was going down the drain. Wow! Talk about being stressed–I was stressed. How could I possibly go in there and try to get them to "lighten up." I rarely get nervous, but I was sure nervous that day.

So, not one to shy away from the truth, I laid it out right at the beginning. I said to them, "I know I'm here to help you all deal with your stress and to help you lighten up, but I'm so sad for you and so worried about what to say to you..." Their response, much to my delight was:

"Hey, it couldn't get any worse–we NEED to lighten up!"

We had a great time. They laughed, played and even learned a few helpful tips. I had a great lesson.

Paradigm: Humor can definitely lighten up anyone's load, so never underestimate its power.

Once again, I rest my case. Everyone go out there and lighten up your workplace–you'll be creating an incredible environment–a place where people will LOVE coming to work, and while they're at work, they'll cope more effectively with change and stress.

**And when they cope better,
you should serve ice cream.**

FIVE

Resiliency…. "Like A Rubber Ball, I Come Bouncing Back To You!"

At the height of laughter, the universe is flung into a kaleidoscope of new possibilities." *Jean Houston*

Lean in close now so you can really hear this: **There's a natural order to all things** … there's wheat before bread, milk before butter, labor before birth, surgery before healing… But what does this mean **to you?**

True mastery can be gained by letting things go their own way. It can't be gained by interfering. *Lao Tzu*

Remember the story about the little kid that's waist deep in manure and covered from head to toe and still smiling. OK, so he's tromping around in this barn full of horse (you know what) and he's having a ball. Finally, someone asks him what he's so happy about and he replies, "With all this manure, there's gotta be a pony in here someplace."

Well, the attitude he's expressing is **RESILIENCY.** Big word! *Resiliency* is the ability to bounce back from whatever is going on. I refer to it as *the human rubber-band syndrome.*

People who are resilient do much better at handling change of any kind. Do you know why? Because they have a number of very valuable characteristics–they're optimistic, persistent, unstoppable, flexible; they're curious, and want to know what's coming around the next corner; they're creative and they LAUGH; they go with the flow; they expect challenges; they expect that life will not be perfect and they know that "stuff" happens; they even expect fear. However, when *it* comes, whatever *it* is, they play at life with childlike enthusiasm, a sense of adventure and creativity. **That creative perspective leads to creative thinking, which can turn life's problems into solutions.**

So, ask yourself–What would it take for me to be more resilient? How can I turn what's seemingly negative or unpleasant to my advantage?

Why is this important you might be wondering? We'll go back to the dichotomy we raised last time–stress and change can create a CRISIS or an OPPORTUNITY. Which do you want?

Things do always change. Just look at some of the changes we've had in our country over the last couple of years. We've seen companies go out of business, companies stay in business and lay off many valuable employees, home sales have begun to slow and prices have taken a bit of a down turn, not to mention the down-up-down turns in the stock market. All of this dwells in the circle of what we call *life.* How well do you handle it?

Author's note

I'd like to share one of my most valuable experiences. In fact, this story is about an event that completely altered my life and brought me to where I am today.

It was a cold day in Austin, in January, 1987 (well, not all *that* cold compared to Minneapolis or Chicago, like maybe 50 degrees). I was the director of an adolescent drug and alcohol program.

Yes, I should really tell you that I actually did meaningful work in those days.

I left my office one day and I nearly burst into tears before I got to my car. For weeks, I'd been crying everyday when I left work. The stress of the job had been taking its toll on me. My future looked bleak and I was miserable.

I was actually a weanie back than…not mature like I am now.

On this one particular day in January, I cried all the way home–I just couldn't stop crying. I knew I was totally burned out, but I didn't know what to do. I pulled into my driveway and into the garage. I looked in the mirror, trying to wipe away the mascara that had run down my cheeks, wanting to look like everything was just fine. I walked into the kitchen. My son, who was then 9, was standing in the middle of the kitchen. He looked at me and said, "Mom, are you going to cry everyday when you come home from work?"

[Wham!! Busted by a 9-year-old! Kids always tell the truth and you can never pull the wool over their eyes.]

I remember, as if it were this morning, putting my hand under his chin, looking him in the eyes and saying, "Life is too short for this." I told him to get his Dad and the three of us went to Showbiz Pizza (which is now Chuckie Cheese). We ate, drank, played games and laughed a lot.

When I got home that night, I sat down at the computer and wrote my letter of resignation. I had no idea what I would do next. Circumstances did not favor my leaving the security of a job, but at that moment–when I looked into my son's eyes–I *knew* what I had to do.

Now if I had been being practical I would never have done that . As it was, I abandoned all practicality and just leapt .. (is that a word?). Might as well let you know who I really am.

The next morning, I turned in my resignation and *I never looked back*!

What happened next was like a miracle. I had never considered working for myself–it wasn't even on the radar screen. I always thought that people worked for others–period–even though salary levels were pitiful in Austin back then.

Not much better now, either.

I didn't have much hope. But, suddenly, people started calling me. They had heard I was "available" and asked me to do some consulting, see some private counseling clients, teach some courses…Everything just fell together in a way that gave me an opportunity to branch off on to my own. And, as I said, I never looked back–I seized the opportunity and I did whatever it took to make my business work.

MORAL: A lot of things that I felt I had no control over had happened. In a single moment, I decided to *choose* to do something different. I did whatever it took and I made it. I found out what a resilient person I am.

End of story.

I could inspire you with lots of stories about resilience–mine and other people's–but I won't. The inspiring point is, whether it's about career satisfaction or more personal issues, it's what you *choose* to do and how you weather the storm. In other words, it is how *resilient* you are, that counts.

In the workplace, when you're riddled with stress and only change and uncertainty lie ahead, it's every decision you make, every moment you take, your willingness to face the issues *head on*, and your ability to *LAUGH* and roll with the punches that will get you through.

There's a wonderful book entitled, *Unstoppable*, by Cynthia Kearsey (see reading list).

In her book, Kearsey lists the seven characteristics of unstoppable people. I've included them here for you.

Unstoppable people:

- ✓ Devote themselves to their true purpose
- ✓ Follow their heart's passion
- ✓ Believe in themselves and their ideas
- ✓ Prepare for challenges
- ✓ Ask for help and build a support team
- ✓ Seek creative solutions
- ✓ Persevere, no matter what the challenges

I'll take the liberty of adding an eighth characteristic: Unstoppable people always remember to laugh and keep their sense of HUMOR intact.

Exercise:

Rate your own resiliency on a scale of 1-10. Be sure to elaborate about some times when you were resilient, particularly at work.

A final note:

The word *humor* comes from the Latin "oomar", which means flexible, like water.

And, water, of course flows .. in a resilient sort of way. So, humor means resilient. Cool!.

"Laughter and play on the job are not an end in and of themselves. They are a doorway, an entrée into being more human with the people we work with … the only way to keep a sense of fun and play in your work life is to consciously choose to make it a priority."

Matt Weinstein

SIX

HUMOR AND MANAGEMENT

I think the next best thing to solving a problem is finding some humor in it."

Frank A. Clark

I might make a few enemies here, but I contend that too many managers are promoted to management without a roadmap of "how" to be a manager.

Does "clueless" fit here?

It's really not their fault. They probably have great technical expertise in their particular field, but they often do not possess management skills.

What if *you* are a manager (experienced or not), and you have to deal with intense changes at work? What do you do? How do you handle it all? First, I'll toss out some ideas for you to consider–kind of a starting point–then we'll get into the nitty-gritty.

✓ Have a clear destination; in other words, *know where you're going.* Begin with the end in mind–if you don't have a map, how will you know how to get there?

✓ Be honest–keep your co-workers and staff members aware of what's happening and how it will affect them. Don't let anyone feel left out.

✓ Honor people's efforts and recognize and reward them for their loyalty. Be sure to acknowledge the fact that they, too, have changes to deal with and acknowledge their courage and contributions.

- ✓ Believe in your people. Help them create and achieve "outside the box", help them be innovative with the changes they face.
- ✓ Thank your staff and celebrate! Celebrations recharge people's batteries and make them feel special and refreshed.

"Talented employees need great managers. How long that employee stays and how productive he is while he is there is determined by his relationship with his immediate supervisor."
Marcus Buckingham and Curt Coffman

First Break All the Rules

Truly Great Managers Like to Have Fun!!

A few years ago, there was a popular Cyndi Lauper song entitled, Girls Just Want To Have Fun. It was kind of a catchy tune–easy to sing and one that kept ringing in your ears.

Actually, it's ringing in my ears now and distracting me. I bet it will start ringing in their ears too. It's catchy.

Well, how about a variation on that? *Employees just want to have fun.* For employees truly to have fun at work, it stands to reason that their managers would have to be at least a little bit fun as well. I mean, even if the manager could be 20% fun, that would be better than 5%. Of course, 50% fun would be even better, but let's not expect miracles...So, think now; if you are a manager, where would you place yourself on a scale of 1–10 in terms of your "fun-ness" level at work? (1 is *I hate fun and never have any,* and 10 is *I love fun, I'm always fun and never have a serious bone in my body.*) If you're an employee, where would you rate your manager according to this scale?

"Fun-ness" Scale

1	**10**
I hate fun and never have any.	***I love fun, I'm always fun and never have a serious bone in my body.***

A huge problem that exists in the workplace today is this dilemma of managing when you "might not" have experience as a manager.

That's being generous... the truth is they're probably clueless

Language is the most important variable. If you're not speaking the same language as your staff, chances are pretty good that the message is **not** getting from the messenger to the recipient. Good eye contact and the ability to listen well are really important, too. Although these are good suggestions for establishing rapport, what about deepening the relationship so you can become a reeeealy good manager?

Some Ideas:

So, what does it take for a manager to be, not just a mediocre manager, but a GREAT manager? First, you have to build rapport with your staff. OK, so how do you build rapport anyway? Well, you find ways to relate to them–not just as workers, but as human beings. When you talk to your staff, make sure you're talking the same language–and I don't just mean *English.* I mean, you want them to receive whatever message you're sending. Right? So you have to have some idea of how they think and you have to be *real*–don't try to con them. Besides that, good eye contact and great listening skills, what else can you do? You can smile and say, "Hi" when you pass people in the corridors or when you pass by someone's desk; you can put on funny glasses or a wig for a staff meeting…

Of course, donuts aren't a bad idea either;

---

you can challenge them to Nerf basketball in the hallway; you can place a trash can in the hallway and have folks make paper airplanes and aim them at the can, or you can stop and tell a joke.

Of course the jokes need to be clean and appropriate, right? I mean, the people reading this would KNOW that, wouldn't they?

Does being FUN make a good manager good? Maybe so, maybe not. Inversely though, if you're a manager and you are at "zero" on the sense of humor or "fun-ness" scale, you probably won't be a good manager. So, if you want to remain a manager and you don't register high on the scale, what are some things you can do?

Let's begin with the morning. When you get to work and have your first meeting of the day, how do you start off? Do you speak in a monotone or do you have some inflection in your voice? Does your hand shake as you hold your coffee cup because you've already had too much caffeine, or are you still in a sleepy zone? Either way, you might want to begin the meeting with a point of good cheer. Say something wonderful about the day, or share a cute story about something that happened at home last night, or create a challenge for the group that day by suggesting that the people or group that do ____ that day will get ____ for a prize. (Make sure the prize is something truly fun.) You might also want to be in costume or wearing a clown nose or some similarly funny prop as people enter the meeting room in the morning. The surprise is sure to bring a few snickers and maybe even laughs.

Of course you have to be willing to look totally ridiculous and have people laugh at you.

As the day continues, get creative. How can you keep folks laughing at work? Find any reason at all to laugh. Show baby pictures or watch a funny video. Or, you can serve a theme lunch–perhaps a "cowboy lunch" or a "biggest sandwich of all time" lunch. Just be creative!

I once served only interesting finger food, without utensils. I served things like meatballs, chocolate pudding. Amazing how many people freaked out and were uncomfortable.

After lunch might be a good time to have a little "jam-min" time. Have everyone bring their favorite (portable) musical instrument. Gather out on a patio and do some jamming, even for just 15 minutes.

You might want to bring your ear plugs ... just in case. I mean I didn't say they had to know how to play, right?

Then, when it's back to work time, you can leave your door open so staff members feel they can approach you with questions or information, or good news–like they did well in the computer programming course you arranged for them. Perhaps when they enter your office, they can pick up a sign from your table that says, "This is a fun/good question" or "This is a serious issue". Or, maybe tell them they have to smile/grin to get your attention or that they have to ring a gong or hit a drum to enter. An open door works really well as opposed to the door that hits them in the "you know where" as they exit. Make your office inviting with pictures, toys, or homey touches like a decorative rug and comfortable chairs.

If you don't want to encourage them … have no chairs in your office for them to sit in or, better yet, just put up a huge Do Not Enter sign.

Now, how do you handle those difficult situations, like when someone makes a mistake? Perhaps handling it the way a kindergarten teacher would. Give gentle, understanding feedback, rather than a scolding. People respond much better to someone giving them concrete, constructive info rather than yelling. You could even hand out gold stars for a job well-done and then give a prize for the most accumulated stars.

Exercise:

Think about what would happen if you used some of these "good management" techniques; What positive impact would it have? What great ideas can you come up with? Be sure to write down your ideas—you may come up with so many, you might forget a few of the best.

Remember, even though employees "just want to have fun", more than that, they want to be appreciated and acknowledged.

Right about now, you might be thinking, "Why do I want to go through all this effort to have fun? Why can't people just do what they're hired to do so the workplace can run efficiently?"

Well, because I wanted to write a book and this is the topic of the moment!

Aha! I have the answer–here it is…Are you ready?

You can't get blood from a turnip, but you can get milk from a cow. And, mixed with chocolate syrup, milk tastes terrifically tasty and satisfying.

Interpretation: If all you do is expect work, work, work where people feel like lifeless automatons (AKA turnips), you will find that you get much less than what you had expected. However, if you allow people to feel as if they have something nourishing to offer (cows), then you gently "milk" them for production; then throw in a little sugar for an added treat…the sky's the limit for what outcomes are possible.

Note: If you strut around in a spotted cow suit, you might get even more.

So, why not manage your staff in such a way that you create an environment that makes people LOVE coming to work each day; so you maximize potential so production is high; and you up the bottom line and the integrity of your company???

Perhaps you might even have fun… what a concept!

Paradigm: Create an environment where people LOVE coming to work!

Managing in Challenging Times and Having a Sense of Humor

A few more thoughts. I didn't think I had enough pages for this chapter, so I made up some more stuff.

Things are getting rougher out there. For many, it may feel like the daily terrain is loaded with landmines. Fortunately, we live in a country where we've not had to experience the horror of actually walking on a landmine–for which I am grateful everyday. But we do live in a country that is experiencing unexpected and unpredictable changes everyday and around every corner.

For several years, we saw a tremendously positive trend in our economy with low unemployment, better salaries, and new companies soaring into the stratosphere almost overnight. Much of that has changed and it suddenly seems as though everything is coming unglued, falling apart, doing a nosedive.

"Ouch! Help! What do I do now? Oh my God! Oh no!" Those are all terms we hear around us these days. How to cope with the unexpected? How to "not fall apart" when it seems the world around us *is* falling apart? A sense of humor, you say? Well, how almost sacrilegious that may sound to some. How can we laugh at hard times? How can we snicker when people are being laid off all around the country? How can we giggle, when people's homes are being foreclosed? I ask, **how can we NOT?**

No one can create or restore our sense of humor for us. We have to find it and tap into it all on our own, by ourselves; and, yes, tap in at whatever rate of speed is comfortable for us–especially in difficult times. Don't let anyone force you into anything any sooner than you're ready and refrain from forcing anyone else to smile or laugh before they are ready. Respect each individual's calendar and internal clock. Some people will want to laugh and make jokes and get back to life very quickly after some professional or personal disaster; and others are barely hanging on. Respect where they are. **MANAGERS: FYI**–this paragraph is for you. Please read it again. Your skills of compassion are being called upon. How will you "be" for your employees? That's easy. Be present to whatever they need and wherever they are.

Also, bringing in some good quality chocolate might help too or a few little toys, or pizza.

What would they like? What would help boost their spirits? Trust yourself; go with your instinct.

Many misunderstand a "sense of humor." They think it means guffawing–laughing all over the place. Well, it doesn't. By *a sense of humor*, I am merely referring to an "attitude." At Humor U, we like to call it your "laughitude"–your laughter/attitude.

Choicepoint

Here's a news flash for you:

I can almost hear the trumpets.

How you feel or react in any moment is up to you–it's your CHOICE. YOU can choose how to react to whatever is going on around you; the reaction doesn't choose you.

Case in point:

This is a test to see how you're doing.

You lose your job. You can get depressed or you can get angry or you can feel like a victim, or you can get into action about searching for another, or you can take a mini-vacation and get yourself relaxed and calm before taking action, or you can move to a deserted island or move in with your parents or kids, or you can do nothing, OR you can laugh and move forward. You see how many choices there are–and I'm certain there are lots more I didn't name.

Remember ... "conscious choosing."

Exercise:

Think of how many more choices would fit the above scenario; Make a list and put it someplace where you can look at it on a regular basis.

Now, what if you're a manager and you're charged with the task of boosting the morale of your work team following a forced layoff of 30% of your company's entire staff–What would you do? How would you handle it?

Let's consider some ways you *could* react: you could hide in your office and not deal with it; you could call everyone in one at a time and express your sorrow and concern; you could call a full (remaining) team meeting and serve ice cream and cake; you could pass the peace pipe.

Containing legal substances of course, and hope it works–you'll probably have to find someplace out of doors to do this. Or, just keep that fire extinguisher close again.

You could quit your job; you could hire someone to help you; you could have a party for those who have been laid off and for those staying–kind of a unity and closure affair. Then, you could equalize yourself with the rest of the team by having a meeting with them all as a fresh start, engaging them in the process of deciding how to proceed.

What does it take to be the kind of manager that truly "serves" your employees; the kind of manager that your employees respect and aspire to be like? Well, it takes one who isn't afraid to be him/herself–to express your own feelings in response to the tough decisions, one who allows others to express their feelings, one who comforts and checks on how they're doing, one who invites ideas for coping.

Okay, Ann... tell them to stop hiding in the closet and just get out there and be great or outrageous or something.

Author's note

I contract with a small company in a nearby community. I've been coaching some of their project managers for some time... helping them be the best they can be. These managers are great AND they'd be the first to admit that they came to management from the arena of being technically great. They're in the process of developing their management and leadership skills.

A time came, not too long ago, when they had to implement layoffs. It was either layoffs OR the company not being able to keep its doors open much longer. They were very nervous about delivering the difficult news. The day came and there was little time to prepare. They each sat with one employee at a time, accompanied by an H.R. representative, to deliver the news.

I was asked to be there for them. Now, sometimes employees being laid off think that the person doing the firing has it easy; after all, *that* person still has a job. Not true. No one likes this process and it's anything but easy.

After they talked to the "chosen" employees…the ones being asked to leave , we gathered in a conference room. We brought in pizza, we got silly, cracked some uncomfortable jokes, and, in between, I let them discuss how hard it was. I had a few toys on the table and a little chocolate. We interspersed the more serious talk with lightheartedness. There was no demand for anyone to share. They chose to talk it out and they chose to laugh a bit–everyone handled it differently.

I was glad I could help and I admired the leadership within for thinking enough of all their employees to include me!

Exercise:

Think about these questions and jot down your answers in your journal: What kind of a manager are you? (Or, what kind of manager do you have?) How do you deal with the landmines—do you step on them or do you artfully and successfully dodge them? What kind of a person are you?

My motto–*When all else fails, use humor.* Laughter will get your blood flowing, and it will create resiliency–the ability to roll with the punches. So, get out your hiking shoes and turn on your humor radar and let's start dodging and laughing!

"Humor instantly took us away, even if only for moments, from our troubles and made them easier to bear. It gave us a breather. It was like a mini-vacation that allowed us to regain our strength and pull our resources together."

Allen Klein

The Healing Power of Humor

SEVEN

How to Teach the Importance of Humor

In order to survive these wild times, you're going to make a total fool of yourself with incredible regularity. If you can't laugh about it...you are doomed.

Tom Peters

It starts with *you.* Before we get to the *how* to teach humor in the workplace, you must first look at your own *Humor Quotient.* On a scale of 1–10, where are *you*?

Humor Quotient

1	**10**
Dead on a slab	***Hilarious, off the chart***

How do you teach another person–a serious other person–to lighten up? It's easy–first, you lighten up yourself.

Author's note

Several years ago, I was hired by a very large corporation to coach one of their upper level executives, who we'll call, "Paul". Paul was on track most likely to assume the role of CEO. Paul was brilliant with an MBA from a prestigious university, young, vital, extremely bright and talented... and while he had all of that, he somewhat lacked in the arena of social skills. What the company wanted me to do was to help him lighten up, become more sociable and develop some "people" skills.

I'd be lying if I said I had a ready-made formula in place to make this man a truly fun-loving, warm, light-hearted person. In spite of the fact that he was likeable, there was just that "something missing". It was really hard to get a handle on it.

Paul and I worked together for several months. At times it was like pulling teeth for me. He couldn't quite put his finger on why he was so different at work from how he was in his personal life. We'd examine his personal life and talk about what generated smiles and laughter for him. He saw himself as a pretty fun loving guy, who laughed a lot, enjoyed being a Dad, husband, and friend. He also saw himself as a great communicator.

At work, however, he had a sense people didn't see him in the same way.

That was obviously true… the CEO hired me to work with him!

We'd discuss how well he knew his staff, how he dressed on casual Fridays, his staff's perception of him. There was much to be done. How would we "transfer" some of how he was personally into how he could/should be professionally? Eventually, we *were* able to transfer some of his personal flair for "lightheartedness" into his work environment. Let me tell you how we did it.

Some "how to's"

I hope they pay attention … this is the "executive FUN coaching" stuff.

What did I do with Paul? Let me try to break it down here step by step.

The first step is to fully assess how humorous and fun-loving a person already is. Since there are no paper and pencil tests for this, I've come up with another way to make an assessment. I assign the person I'm working with the task of asking everyone they can think of to answer the question, "How much fun am I to be around?"

What we're going after here is their ***humor quotient.*** The person asking the question tells everyone he or she asks to be totally honest because they *really* want to know. They have to ask a broad range of people–people from work, spouses, children and other family members, friends and other people they interact with in their personal lives. And, it's very important that they really be willing to *hear* what the others are saying and not try to alter or sway the person's response in any way. This is reality testing–finding out exactly how much fun others think you are, *even if you don't really want to know.*

Author's note

I'll tell one on myself here. People who know me really well know that I am a *recovering serious person*; yes, it's true, I have a strong serious side. In fact, at first, a lot of my friends thought I had found a new interpretation for the word "humor" when I told them I was going to teach about humor in the workplace–they couldn't believe that serious me was going to teach people how to use fun!.

I always had a love of acting–was even in some amateur theatre–so, when I'm in front of a room, training or speaking, it's easy for me to convey real joy and fun. But, even though I have come to really believe in humor and having fun, when I have weighty things on my mind, I can be pretty serious, too. So you see, you really need to have the people who answer your "...how funny am I..." question be 100% honest, keeping in mind all aspects of you. So, whether you like the answers you get or not, *truth* is vital if you're going to learn how to lighten up!

The second step is to share the results of this survey with someone who is a mentor or significant person in your life. Let that person help you look for differences between how you are inside and outside of work and among different communities of people; this will tell you a lot about your comfort zone. You really want to get this … even if it's a little unpleasant.

Step three is to begin to transfer skills from one setting to another. So, if you're great fun when romping around with your kids on a Saturday afternoon, then how can we take some of that energy and put it into your interactions with people at work? This is the tricky part. No, I'm not suggesting that you crawl around on the floor with your workmates, but you can *learn to enjoy* being with certain people and, when you're with them, behave in a way that's similar in feeling to when you're clowning around with your kids or friends. The key is that the clowning around needs to be appropriate to the situation you are in with the other people. Does that make sense? You're transferring some of the behavior patterns that are fun into a situation where you wouldn't have thought of having fun before–get it?? ***Transferring behavior***. Then, over time, you practice new ways of being. For example, let's say you never dressed down on casual Fridays before; so, now you do. Or, let's say you weren't very conversational with some of your peers before; now you are. See? By transferring behaviors you engage in with friends or family into the workplace, the result is a different behavior pattern–in this case, a more light-hearted, humorous pattern.

Once you spend some time practicing Step 3–for a month, let's say–the fourth and final step is to re-assess how fun you are now compared to before. Ask the same people the same question as before. Once again, it's time for a reality check of your progress. If you've made progress, fantastic! You're on the right track and keep it up. Do you need to keep working at it? Okay, go through the steps again.

So, does it make sense? Yes, but you might ask, "How *long* is this going to take?" There is only one honest answer–*as long as it takes.* I've worked one on one with some folks for a couple of months and with others for over a year. For each person, it's a learning process–and eventually, each person figures out how to lighten up. They do when they do! Isn't that what we call *en**lighten**ment*?

So, these are some of my ideas and some of my processes. Think about your own. Do what comes naturally for you. Haven't you ever helped a friend lighten up a bit?

I know, give him a beer.

No, that's not quite what I mean. I bet you take a friend to an activity, like a sports game, or a movie or to hear some music or shopping or whatever. You find a way to change their mood a bit so that they feel different. That's really what it's all about. Simple?!!

Exercise:

Ask yourself "What do I do to help others lighten up? How about me—how do I help myself lighten up?

So, once again, how can you create an environment where your employees will feel happy at work?

An initial step is to select a "designated fun person"–someone who is normally a happy, fun, and playful person. Then, ask that person to select a Workplace FUN committee. Then, let the committee create your FUN workplace.

Once again, a fun workplace is one where employees can:

- ✓ be openly lighthearted
- ✓ laugh out loud, even in the hallways
- ✓ post funny pictures and cartoons and have contests
- ✓ have "dress down" days and "theme" days
- ✓ have toys on their desks and music in their offices
- ✓ have secret pals and give surprise gifts to each other
- ✓ bring their pet dogs, cats or fish to work and even to meetings
- ✓ have a break room that really gives them a break–with paints and easels, audiotapes, funny videos, comic books and more–so they return to their desks refreshed and ready to work.

Remember, one of our mottos at Humor U is, ***"the company that plays together, stays together!"***

Paradigm: Happy employees are productive employees! The more lighthearted the workplace, the better the performance level, the better the results! The better the results...the more $ you save, the more $ you make. It's that simple!

"Adults are just grown-up kids. We don't grow out of our need for acknowledgement, acceptance, fun and play. We fool ourselves into thinking that to be an adult means to be serious when all it really means is to have aged."

Dave Hemsath and Leslie Yerkes

EIGHT

Creativity and improvisation: Look at What We Can Create– Humor and Creative Thought

Wit is the sudden marriage of ideas which, before their union, were not perceived to have any relation.
Mark Twain

Humor is an awesome and underused business tool.
Tom Peters

At a workshop recently, during a Q & A session, I was asked a couple of great questions.

"Hey, Ann," one Coach asked, "How do you use humor to spark creative thought?"

Someone else asked, "Ann, how do you make sure that humor is used appropriately?"

I thought the questions were really good ones and decided to include both topics in my book. So, here goes.

Well, here I go making stuff up again. But if they're still reading, it must be good "made up" stuff.

Let's look at what creativity means. Good old *Webster's Collegiate Dictionary* defines *creativity* as *...inventive or imaginative*. So, I guess that means that if one is being creative, they have a good imagination and can conjure up unique thoughts or ideas. Sounds plausible to me.

When you think about who is truly imaginative, who comes into your mind right away? For me, it's children and animals. They know how to turn anything into a play toy and then, of course, they play with it. It doesn't matter if it's a wad of paper that someone else tossed aside or an empty box that once held Cheerios or a pile of dirt. They will find more ways than one to transform whatever object they find into something fun and pleasure producing. Wow!! Can you still do that? If not, spend an afternoon on a playground and watch the dogs and the kids. You'll catch on quickly.

It's regrettable that, as we grow up, we often lose our more imaginative powers; but what happens to them? Where do they go? In some cases, they get knocked out of us by ridicule; or we believe that we are supposed to develop a sense of seriousness to go along with more demanding educational requirements or professional demeanor. So our imaginative powers just float to the back burner of our brains. How many of you were taught that you couldn't (weren't allowed to) play until all your work was done? What's the problem with that idea? Right–work is never really *done.* So, we keep our nose to the grindstone and get more and more serious and less and less imaginative and creative.

Nose to the grindstone…sounds pretty scary and dangerous to me.

Personally, I like my nose just the way it is and just where it is.

So, what about creativity in the workplace? What form does it take? What about the concept of "brainstorming?" How often are you called upon to brainstorm? Probably, a lot. Some people intensely dislike brainstorming. Why? Because when they offer their thoughts they frequently get *shot down* (that's where the "ridicule" comes in). It doesn't take too many of those experiences to turn creative risk-taking into a nightmare.

I'd like to share the basic foundation of improvisation (AKA *improv*) and adapt it to brainstorming. It will give you a whole new way to allow for creative thought. Remember, those powers of imagination and creativity that floated to the back burner of your brain–they didn't really leave you. They're still there.

In fact, they're screaming to get out.

Improv is based on the concept of "yes, and." If you watch an improv company on stage, you'll see that they always "go" with whatever the person before them has suggested–they roll with it; they don't obstruct it. So, if someone says, "Let's play baseball," the improv person will say, "Yes, let's play baseball and..." then they add to it. So, they'd say something like, "Yes, and let's form a new team..." and the next person says, "Yes, and let's get a sponsor..." and the next one says, "Yes, and let's go out to Harry's Pub after the game..." You get the drift, right?

At Humor U, we teach companies how to brainstorm using this very same improv concept. Whenever someone throws out an idea, it should be "yes'd" and added to with another suggestion (NEVER squelch or reject anyone's thought). When you master the improv technique in the workplace, you will see those imaginative powers fly from the back burner to the frontal lobe in a hurry–people will start to be creative beyond your wildest imagination. They will get in gear with awesome and fun ideas. It's like a Treasure Chest will open up and out will spill ideas, thoughts, acts, deeds, jokes, comedy, and, maybe even, a gymnastic feat. Amazing! It brings out the child (the most uninhibited creative part of us) in us all and, what's most important to a company, it usually brings out the BEST of ideas because folks are free to associate anything with anything. Voilá–invention takes place! Makes sense, doesn't it?

You know all these little comments I've had scattered throughout the book? Well, they've been improvisational thoughts…random thoughts I put in for my own amusement and yours (hopefully). I just threw them in as I wrote…just for fun. Improvisation really is simple. Try it. Take the fun thoughts out of your head and have them come out of your mouth.

Exercise:

Try this. Get a few people together and create the following, using the "yes, and" concept. Design a new advertising campaign for a new product.
Step 1: Brainstorm a really cool/ fun product (something that doesn't currently exist).
Step 2: Brainstorm another function for this product in addition to the one you already created. Be really imaginative.
Step 3: Decide what famous person would be a great spokesperson for your product.
Step 4: Come up with a slogan for your product.

Ta DA! You have a whole new item. And, I bet you can do it all in 3 minutes. That's what creativity and humor are all about.

So, in a nutshell, *improvisational brainstorming* means you agree to whatever is suggested and then add more to it. Eventually a couple of ideas get dropped as new ones tumble out. Ultimately, there will be an "aha!" and the group will know they've settled on one or two good ideas–and no one shot anything down; instead, they allowed something creative to evolve.

Now, on to the second question–How to make sure that humor is used appropriately.

For humor to work at work, or anyplace really, there has to be some ground rules. The whole idea is for something to be funny or to bring a chuckle; but the goal is to produce a shift in perspective. Humor changes perspective; remember? Humor increases our options and gets us to see something differently.

So, humor needs to be fair, and related. Something said or done to hurt someone or ridicule or make fun of them is NOT humor–it's just plain mean. Therefore, rules have to be established up front. For example, jokes must not put down any group, nor should they use offensive language. The best jokes are the ones people tell about themselves or that make fun of all of us–people in general, with no one singled out. Example: "Half the people like to work and the other half don't, or maybe it's the other way 'round!"

I know, rules can be a royal pain... but they keep you from getting sued...so you might not want to complain

---

To unite the two topics, let me summarize like this: Using humor in brainstorming MUST be for the purpose of expanding perspective, encouraging powers of creative thought and imagination, and creating a lighthearted environment. Humor must NEVER be used to criticize, ridicule or somehow "make wrong" anyone else's ideas

---

The point... You want to open people up, not shut them down.

So, in order for this to work, all humor must be considered appropriate by EVERYONE.

End of lecture!

Humor and creativity go hand in hand even when the brainstorming is about serious topics. Remember, it's a way to create a new perspective and produce outcomes in a non-threatening way. It works. Try it!

IMPROV–Thinking on Your Feet

The qualities of rapport-building, communication and connectedness are what's desired–in fact, desperately *needed*–in today's workplace. So, what does that entail? It means we need skills that enable us to think outside the box like brainstorming, team building, creativity, cooperation, flexibility…All of these skills are incorporated in the skills of improv–improvisation–the art of being spontaneous or "in the moment," and "thinking on your feet."

Here are some ways to apply improv techniques in the workplace. Again, these were developed by my business associate Terrill Fischer.

✓ **Change**: The buzzwords for the 21st Century are *constant change.* Improv disrupts patterned, rigid or conditioned thinking and allows for greater flexibility.

✓ **Creativity & Innovation**: Improv helps to generate new ideas and gets us thinking outside the box. This helps us become more innovative with our thinking. We can learn brainstorming techniques that take us places we've never been before and never thought we could or would go. It's amazing how our ability to think in big picture ways provides limitless possibilities.

✓ **Team Work**: Improv is all about working together with others to create group harmony and establish rapport among the people with whom you work. Don't play "serious" survival games; instead, play fun, consensus building games, designed to facilitate collaboration and teamwork.

- ✓ **Stress Management**: Improv helps to lighten the load from the stressors of the workplace such as downsizing, doing more with less, re-engineering, and the everyday demands on your time. Try "downloading" your stress, shipping it off on the wings of paper airplanes, dancing it away with music, and any other way that is active and fun.
- ✓ **Problem Solving**: Improv is about overcoming challenges and looking for new approaches to create the results you want.
- ✓ **Decision-Making**: Improv requires coming up with fast decisions or thinking quickly on the spot or on your toes–very important skills for the workplace.
- ✓ **Communication**: Improv incorporates the skills of listening, responding, speaking, observation, cooperation, and authenticity. All necessary skills, right? You bet!
- ✓ **Trust**: Improv builds on the ability to work comfortably and confidently with other people, thus bonding people together and creating a trusting environment.

Do you want to get better at improv? Want to know more about it and how to do it? All you need to do is find your local improv comedy club and sign up for a class. You can attend performances too, but taking a class and really *doing it* is how you'll learn. It will challenge you and take you to levels you never knew you could reach; and it will definitely bring out your sense of humor.

The paths to creativity and improvisation … are the same path!

Be in the Moment!

The idea is:

Why should children have all the fun? Fun is good for your head, your heart, your spirit, your blood pressure, your sex life. Let loose more often. Surprise, delight, laughter are nectar to the gods; play is the ultimate prayer. Give yourself a break, take time off from worrying, soul-searching, trying so hard. The circus is in town; watch the clowns, whose job it is to knock us on our backsides, and make us guffaw at the comedy of being human. Be silly for a change. Try to remember what children haven't yet forgotten.

From O Magazine May 2002

NINE

A Few Last Words

Yeah, that'll be the day!

I don't want to patronize you by doing an entire summary here. I know you can read and you've heard many of the messages of this book ... over and over in the last 8 chapters.

What I do want to do, however, is somehow pull it all together and close this baby out.

Humor produces many benefits: It frees communication, changes perspective, empowers, acts as a connector, decreases tension and ...it facilitates learning and performing!

And, of course, humor makes people laugh. Bottom line: Add a little humor to your place of work and you will have increased productivity, higher retention of your best employees and a place where people are actually inspired to work! Yes, you'll have a spirited workplace.

Remember.... Ka ching? Yep... this is the part where we see... more $$$

So, I ask you ... what are you going to be doing differently now that you KNOW, definitively, that humor at work works?

Are you going to say, "ho hum" and keep on doing what you've been doing? You know what they say about that ... "If you do what you've always done, you'll get what you've always got." Or "If nothing changes, nothing changes."

This would not be a the right choice!

I know you'll be making those changes I'm suggesting. In fact, I assume that if I were to visit your workplace today and then again in 30 days, it won't even seem like the same place. I just know that you'll have your "designated FUN person" appointed.

Including business cards for him/her… yes, there must be business cards that say "Designated FUN person". Oh, and there will be frufru colors and textures, and a really cool breakroom, and lots of toys and chocolate all around and …..I'm starting to get carried away. Sorry!

I also know that you'll have your FUN committee selected. That committee, by the way, should consist of a blend of all levels, from upper to middle management, to line workers. You want a mixed committee to represent everyone's needs fairly.

I invite you to email me or call me and tell me about the changes you're making at work as a result of reading this book. Inquiring minds want to know and that means ME. If you come up with new ideas, share them with me and I'll share them with the whole world out there, through my Humor Tips e-newsletter.

Ann@HumorU.com

And yes, of course I'll give you all the credit. I'm really pretty nice that way!

FIVE

Resiliency.... "Like A Rubber Ball, I Come Bouncing Back To You!"

At the height of laughter, the universe is flung into a kaleidoscope of new possibilities." *Jean Houston*

Lean in close now so you can really hear this: **There's a natural order to all things** ... there's wheat before bread, milk before butter, labor before birth, surgery before healing... But what does this mean **to you?**

True mastery can be gained by letting things go their own way. It can't be gained by interfering. *Lao Tzu*

Remember the story about the little kid that's waist deep in manure and covered from head to toe and still smiling. OK, so he's tromping around in this barn full of horse (you know what) and he's having a ball. Finally, someone asks him what he's so happy about and he replies, "With all this manure, there's gotta be a pony in here someplace."

Well, the attitude he's expressing is **RESILIENCY.** Big word! *Resiliency* is the ability to bounce back from whatever is going on. I refer to it as *the human rubber-band syndrome.*

People who are resilient do much better at handling change of any kind. Do you know why? Because they have a number of very valuable characteristics–they're

In the words, once again, of Dr Seuss:

"Congratulations!
Today is your day.
You're off to Great Places!
You're off and away.

You have brains in your head.
You have feet in your shoes.
You can steer yourself
Any direction you choose.

Dr. Seuss

Make today the day!! Laugh a lot... because... Laughing Truly Does Matter!!!

Now, go out and make the world an even better place. I'm counting on you and so is everyone else.

Thanks and good luck!

Well, actually, luck has nothing to do with it. I mean if it did, we'd just rely on luck all the time, but we know that we have to be the ones to make things happen and can't just rely on the fates and the luck thing. I mean that's just "woo woo" thinking again, Ann. They don't really want to hear that. You've done your talking, you've shown your weird side, now just say "never mind" like Emily Latella and stop talking.

The End

APPENDIX

A few important things you might be interested in:

DAILY "TAKE STOCK" SHEET

(Ask yourself these questions and answer them every day)

1. What were the things I did today that made me laugh?

2. How many times or for how many minutes did I laugh today?

3. What were the things I did today that made other people laugh?

4. What experiences did I treasure today?

5. What new information did I learn today?

6. What "learning experiences" or "breakthrough awarenesses" did I have today?

7. What were the things I did to help others today?

8. What "gifts" did I give to others?

9. What "gifts" did I receive today from others?

10. How did I further forward my purpose today?

11. Based on today, what steps do I want to /need to plan for tomorrow?

HUMOR DIAGNOSIS QUESTIONS:

Discovering the "Owies" in your Corporation.

Ordinarily, the staff of Humor U comes into a company and conducts a free assessment/diagnosis. This is the questionnaire we use. How about using it on yourself? For a discussion about how you're doing, you can contact us at www.humoru.com.

Good luck! Please heed what you learn.

Corporate Body questions

1. What works here? – Where is your company the healthiest?
2. What's not working –Where is the disease in your company – where are the **"owies?"** Are they real or hypochondria**?**
3. What bandaids, resuscitation methods, cures, panaceas, placebos have your tried? Have they worked?
4. Are employees encouraged to bring in creative and FUN ideas to improve and "lighten up" the company? Is the company open to their ideas? Are their ideas implemented?
5. Who is the designated "fun person?" Do you have a "fun committee?" What are some of the fun things you do with employees? What do you celebrate?
6. Who are your number one customers? (please respond)
   Sanitation workers?
   The hospital down the street?
   Your clients?
   Your employees?
   Your board members?

Your shareholders?
The IRS?
Your vendors?

(We assume that your employees are your number one customers, so when you look at your employee base, do you see more healthy employees or more dysfunctional/ unhealthy employees?)

7. **What does it cost you** in morale to have unhappy, poorly-functioning employees? What does it cost you in decreased productivity – your bottom line?
8. What's the overall mood or general tenor of your organization?

1	**10**
Dead/ on a slab	***Top Cardio shape***

Management Questions:

1. What's your retention rate vs. your turnover rate (In other words, they're staying for the donuts or they're walking out the door and not coming back).
2. **What does it cost you** every time an employee leaves and you have to hire and/or retrain a replacement? (Re-training means jumping through hoops. Are there circus performers at your site?)
3. How many stress-related symptoms do you see in your workplace?
   a. Are more employees going to the doctor with "owies?"
   b. Are things falling all over the place – accidents?
   c. Are there lots of "blue Monday" absences? All in all would most of your staff *rather be fishing* or getting a flu shot?
4. Do managers frequently complain about employees undermining their decisions?

5. How do your employees work together in teams?

1	**10**
Teams? **What teams?**	***Bonded like glue***

6. What have you tried in the past to make your workplace better. Have you used consulting services or some other service? Do you think it worked to make things better? Do the employees think it made things better? If so, for how long?
7. Does your company need a change? Does it want to change? Is the company currently on crutches and does it want to learn to walk, or to run?

CEO Questions:

1. What would your bottom line be like if your employees were satisfied, felt heard and acknowledged, and **LOVED** coming to work for you everyday because your company is **a FUN** place to be?
2. If you brought in **someone who could really "fix the owies"** (and I don't mean cover them with bandaids) and get your bottom line to look like you want it to (as in #16), what would it be worth to you?
3. What would your desired results be? In other words, what do you really want to see made better here?
4. Can you already see some ways that we can help???

Thanks for taking the time to consider your current situation and see the potential for your company's future!! We look forward to serving you.

Designed and distributed by Humor University, www.humoru.com

FUN FACTS, DID YOU KNOW.....?"*

- It takes 13 muscles to smile and 50 muscles to frown? So, avoid facial wrinkles – SMILE
- Laughter boosts the immune system by decreasing the level of cortisol, an immune suppressor in the body.
- Hearty laughter speeds up the heart rate, improves blocked circulation, accelerates breathing and increases oxygen consumption
- Laughing for 15 seconds adds two days to your life span
- Laughing 100 times a day is equal to a 10-minute session of rowing. So, why sweat when you can laugh?

* FUN FACTS provided by the Library of Life, Love and Laughter, Ball Memorial Hospital, Muncie, Indiana

SOURCES OF STRESS IN THE WORKPLACE*

Job-Related Stressors

- Unfair promotional practices
- Intimidating, demanding management styles
- Conflicts with co-workers/supervisors
- Feeling unqualified to complete an assignment
- Feeling overwhelmed by work
- Lacking support from management
- Poor time management
- Boredom

Environmental Stressors

- Excessive noise
- Non-supportive management
- Unfair rating procedures
- Lack of variety in daily routine
- Failure to receive feedback or recognition
- Unsafe working conditions
- Overcrowded conditions
- Conflicts between employees

Psychological Stressors

- Feeling hopeless or bored
- Too much or too little to do
- Low self-esteem
- High self-criticism
- Lost sense of purpose
- Feeling overwhelmed
- Feeling not in control of self
- Frequent work or job changes
- Communication difficulties

Physical Symptoms of Stress

- Headaches
- Fatigue
- Increased consumption of alcohol, nicotine, or coffee
- Sleep disturbances
- Avoidance or withdrawal
- Moodiness or irritability
- Feeling helpless, trapped in a job

•from "Stress in the Workplace" by Thomas W. Miller, Douglas Jones and Jeanine M. Miller. Published in EAP Digest, May/June 1992.

SUGGESTED READINGS / RESOURCES

Autry, James A. LOVE AND PROFIT: The Art of Caring Leadership. 1991. New York: Avon Books.

Blanchard, Ken. RAVING FANS: A Revolutionary Approach to Customer Service. 1993: New York: William Morrow and Company, Inc.

Bracey, Hyler, et.al. MANAGING FROM THE HEART. 1990. New York: A Dell Trade Paperback.

Buckingham, Marcus and Curt Coffman. FIRST, BREAK ALL THE RULES: What the World's Greatest Managers Do Differently. 1999. New York: Simon & Schuster.

Byham, William C. ZAPP!: THE LIGHTNING OF EMPOWERMENT. 1989. Pittsburgh, PA: Development Dimensions International Press.

Cooper, Robert K. THE OTHER 90%: How to Unlock Your Vast Untapped Potential for Leadership and Life. 2001. New York: Crown Business.

Cousins, Norman. ANATOMY OF AN ILLNESS. 1991. New York: Bantam Books

Covey, Stephen R. PRINCIPLE-CENTERED LEADERSHIP. 1992. New York: A Fireside Book.

Covey, Stephen R. THE SEVEN HABITS OF HIGHLY EFFECTIVE PEOPLE. 1989. New York: A Fireside Book.

Crum, Thomas S. THE MAGIC OF CONFLICT. 1987. New York: Simon & Schuster.

Frieberg, Kevin and Jackie. NUTS: Southwest Airlines' Crazy Recipe for Business and Personal Success. 1996. New York: Broadway Books

Glanz, Barbara A. CARE PACKAGES FOR THE WORKPLACE: Dozens of Little Things You Can Do To Regenerate Spirit at Work. 1996. New York: McGraw Hill.

Goleman, Daniel. EMOTIONAL INTELLIGENCE. 1995. New York: Bantam Books.

Goleman, Daniel. WORKING WITH EMOTIONAL INTELLIGENCE. 2000. New York: Bantam Books.

Harvey, Jerry B. THE ABILENE PARADOX: And Other Meditations on Management. 1988. New York: Lexington Books.

Hemsath, Dave and Leslie Yerkes. 301 WAYS TO HAVE FUN AT WORK. 1997. San Francisco, CA: Berrett-Koehler Publishers, Inc.

Jaworski, Joseph. SYNCHRONICITY: The Inner Path of Leadership. 1996. San Francisco, CA: Berrett-Koehler Publishers.

Johnson, Spencer, M.D. WHO MOVED MY CHEESE? 1998. New York: G.P. Putnam's Sons.

Klein, Allen. THE HEALING POWER OF HUMOR. 1989. Los Angeles: Jeremy P. Tarcher, Inc.

Laborde, Genie Z. INFLUENCING WITH INTEGRITY: Management Skills for Communication and Negotiation. 1986. Syntony Publishing.

Lundin, Stephen, Ph.D, et. al FISH: A Remarkable Way to Boost Morale and Improve Results, 2000. Hyperion.

MacKenzie, Gordon. ORBITING THE GIANT HAIRBALL. 1998: New York: Viking/ Penguin Group.

Nelson, Bob. 1001 WAYS TO REWARD EMPLOYEES. 1994. New York: Workman Publishing.

Rubin, Ron and Stuart Avery Gold. SUCCESS @ LIFE: How to Catch and Live Your Dream. 2001. New York: Newmarket Press.

Ruiz, Don Miguel. THE FOUR AGREEMENTS. 1997. San Rafael, CA: Amber-Allen Publishing, Inc.

Weinstein, Matt. MANAGING TO HAVE FUN. 1996. New York: A Fireside Book.

Wright, Tim. BATTERIES INCLUDED: HOW TO CHARGE AND RECHARGE YOUR CREATIVE CELLS. 2003. Andover, MN: Expert Publishing, Inc.

Zander, Rosamund Stone and Benjamin Zander. THE ART OF POSSIBILITY: Transforming Professional and Personal Life. 2000: Harvard Business School Press.

ABOUT ANN FRY

Ann Fry, MSW, President and Dean of Fun of Humor University, has a background as a psychotherapist. For the past 15 years she has been a corporate trainer, professional speaker and coach. She holds a Master's degree in Social Work from the University of Illinois, is a graduate of Coach University, and holds a Professional Certified Coach (PCC) designation through the International Coach Federation. Ann combines her therapist's knowledge, management experience and sense of humor to create her programs.

She has co-authored, When Was The Last Time You...? and 139 Ways to Lighten Up the Workplace and authored Holiday Management 101. Ann is a professional member of the National Speaker's Association (NSA) and is past-President of the NSA Heart of Texas chapter in Austin, TX.

As a coach, Ann works with managers/executives to "lighten up", be their best and be human in their approach to working with employees. She helps people manage their stress, build their people skills, balance their lives and, most importantly, have a healthy sense of humor.

Ann travels around the country to deliver her programs. While on the road, Ann conducts coaching sessions by phone; and when not traveling, she teaches and coaches over the phone from her home office, maybe even in her pajamas. Perhaps her greatest accomplishment, however, is that she is the mother of Gabriel Fry, an up-and-coming singer. Remember the name–he'll be famous soon!

MENU OF SERVICES

Speaking – Keynote Topics:

- Laughing Matters: The Value of Humor at Work
- Lighten Up: A Playful Approach to Stress Management
- Staying Afloat in a Sea of Change and Keeping Your Sense of Humor Intact
- "Aw, What the Heck.....Do It Anyhow!"

Training

- How to Lighten Up Your Workplace
- Coaching Your Managers To Be Their BEST
- Teams in Crisis: Creating FUN Workteams

Executive/ ManagerialCoching Assessments

The Birkman Method
Humor Diagnosis

Products

Books and tapes
To order, go to www.humoru.com
To contact Ann...
ann@humoru.com
www.annfry.com
512-342-1077

ORDER FORM

Quantity	1-50	51-99	100+
Price Each	$17.97	$15.00	$12.00

Laughing Matters ____ Copies x $ ____= $______

Shipping & Handling $ ________
Texas Sales Tax 8.25% $ ________
Total (US Dollars Only) $ ________

SHIPPING & HANDLING

Quantity	1-5	6- 50	51-100	100+
Charge	$3.00	$7.00	$13.00	FREE

Name ____
Title ____
Organization ______________________________________
Shipping Address __________________________________
Billing Address ____________________________________
City ______________ State _____Zip Code ___________
Email ____
Phone ____

Charge Your Order:
MasterCard Visa Am Express
Credit Card Number ______________________________
Exp. Date ____________
Signature ______________________________________

Make checks payable to:
Humor U
PO Box 300567
Austin, TX 78703

www.humoru.com
Fax: (512) 342-1077
Phone: (512) 342-1077